An INSTRUCTOR'S GUIDE to
Teaching Children to RIDE

An INSTRUCTOR'S GUIDE to
Teaching Children to RIDE

MELISSA TROUP BA, BHSII SM

J.A. Allen
London

© Melissa Troup 2010

First published in Great Britain in 2010

ISBN 978-0- 85131-971-1

J.A. Allen
Clerkenwell House
Clerkenwell Green
London EC1R 0HT

www.allenbooks.co.uk

J.A. Allen is an imprint of Robert Hale Limited

A catalogue record for this book is available from the British Library

Design by del norte (Leeds) ltd
Photographs by, or property of, the author, except for the cover,
p. 57 and p.69 (top) which are by Horsepix
Artwork by Carole Vincer
Edited by Martin Diggle

Printed in China

CONTENTS

CONTENTS

ACKNOWLEDGEMENTS

With thanks to everyone who agreed to have their photos printed, both in the UK and Hong Kong, the latter with kind permission of the Hong Kong Jockey Club. Many thanks also to the BEF for allowing an extract from their Child Protection Policy to be printed, and to the Pony Club for allowing the printing of an excerpt of their rules for the Pony Club Mounted Games.

INTRODUCTION

This book aims to give a basic, but comprehensive guide to teaching children to ride. Most children learn to ride from a love of horses and ponies. From their very first visit to the yard, it is important that we nurture this in order for them not only to become accomplished riders, but to be sympathetic riders also. As children progress, we hope that their interest continues to grow. We, as instructors, can offer them the opportunities to develop their riding and stable management skills in the direction they wish to go, to the benefit of their ponies as well as themselves.

1

Before the first lesson

Information exchanged at the time of booking

Often parents will book lessons after being shown around the yard. The tour should be given by an articulate member of staff, who is able to give a positive impression of the centre, and answer the basic questions which will inevitably be raised. Usually enquiries occur at the weekend, so weekend receptionists/yard staff need to be fully versed regarding taking bookings, prices and information that is required and must be given. Attention to these details reflects positively on the centre and will help ensure that the child arrives on time, correctly clothed, ready to start the lesson.

Information required

This information is normally taken on a Rider Registration form, which usually includes a disclaimer from the centre, and suggests that individual insurance is sought. It should also explain the centre's cancellation policy. The form must be completed, signed and dated by the parent, guardian or carer of the child before booking a lesson.

Information sought should include:
- Name and contact details.
- Emergency contact details.
- Age of rider, height and weight.
- Any previous riding experience.
- Physical condition or learning disability that may affect the child's welfare/safety.

Often, at the end of such forms there is a space for the assessing instructor to fill in the details of riding ability, suitability of mount and suggested course of lessons.

INFORMATION GIVEN

- Minimum age (for many centres, this is 4 years; for some it is 6 years).
- Reassurance of insurance, licence, approval from the British Horse Society, Association of British Riding Schools or Riding for the Disabled. (These certificates must also be displayed in the centre).
- Types of lessons – private, semi-private, group (including size); lesson duration.
- Facilities – indoor schools and outdoor arenas, jumping fields, horses and ponies.
- Instructors' qualifications.
- Opportunities – Pony Club centre, Riding Club centre, competitions, etc.
- Directions to the centre.
- Cancellation period required.
- Suitable clothing.
- Cost of lessons. It is a good idea to give this information last, having first told the prospective client about what your centre has to offer.

CLOTHING

Information regarding appropriate clothing is particularly important since it will help pupils to ride in increased safety and comfort.

HATS

Wearing the correct hat is imperative for safety, and to conform with insurance requirements. The minimum marks and numbers required by a British Horse Society (BHS) riding school at the time of writing are:

- British Kitemark
- CE Stamp
- PAS015 and/or (BS)EN1384 (the 'BS'/British Standard – this does not appear on every make, and is not necessary for insurance.)

The additional current number is: ASTMF1163. This number is insufficient on its own.

Obsolete standards are:

- BS6473 (1984)
- BS4472 (1988)

Prices of hats vary because of points of design detail (such as ventilation) and fashion, rather than actual safety, so there is no need for a parent to break the bank. A jockey skull cap allows the wearer to choose a coloured silk of their choosing. Often, 'velvet' hats tend to have a slightly more oval shape than other types, allowing for variation in head shape.

With regard to price, warn parents against purchasing a second-hand hat as the impact history is unknown, and they are often sub-standard.

Most saddlery shops (including those at riding centres) will have a qualified 'hat fitter' to advise on suitability and fit. It is important to have the hat fitted correctly, not only for reasons of safety, but also because hats are non-returnable. Many centres will lend hats to beginners. When a hat is borrowed from the riding school, an instructor can advise on the points of fitting a hat, but do not take responsibility for actually fitting the hat, unless you are qualified to do so.

Points of advice for fitting a hat are:
- It must fit snugly – there should be no movement either forwards or backwards, or laterally.
- It must cover the forehead and sit just above the eyebrows and ears.
- It must cover the back of the head.
- There must be space for one finger at the back of the hat.
- It must be held in place by correct adjustment of the three- or four-point harness.
- The chinstrap must lie beneath the jaw, and be sufficiently snug that it could not slip forwards and rise above the chin towards the lips.

SHOES
Some centres have a good selection of boots for hire or loan. If not, recommend a shoe like an old-fashioned school shoe with a flat sole and small heel. Trainers and wellies are not suitable as neither has a suitable sole or heel. Also, the former do not protect the toes if accidentally trodden on, and welly tops can snag under the saddle flaps.

BODY PROTECTOR
Again, some centres loan these. Always recommend that a correctly fitted body protector is advisable, but, unlike the hat, it is not mandatory for insurance purposes. As with hats, body protectors should fit snugly, with as much of the back covered as possible, without it touching the saddle when sitting on the pony.

A correctly fitting hat.

TROUSERS

Long trousers should be worn. Leggings or close-fitting jogging bottoms are better than jeans, which have an inside seam that can rub. Once the child has committed to continuing riding, advise purchasing jodhpurs, which can be relatively inexpensive.

TOP

Dress should be appropriate to time of year. If lessons take place in an outdoor school, advise that the child will be subjected to the weather, so waterproofs or sun cream may be necessary at different times. Vest tops are unsuitable, and the top should ideally have long sleeves. Avoid clothing that may rustle (e.g. some waterproofs) and ensure that any jacket can be done up to prevent it from flapping around. Scarves and jewellery should not be worn.

Correctly dressed for riding.

GLOVES

The use of appropriate gloves should be advised all year round, and these are certainly necessary in winter, as little hands become cold quickly when movement is relatively limited. However, unless they have grip, gloves make holding the reins more difficult. Relatively inexpensive, 'pimple palm' gloves could mean the difference between a child enjoying their riding, and being too cold. These gloves are also useful to enhance grip in wet conditions.

FACTORS AFFECTING LESSON TIME

GROUP LESSONS

For groups aged 4 to 6, half an hour is sufficient in terms of both physical and mental stamina.

From the age of 6, children begin to become physically stronger and start to receive mental training at school, and can therefore concentrate for longer periods. Group lessons of up to an hour are suitable for children from 6 to 8 years upwards. With children aged 6-8, gradually build stamina with frequent breaks. Breaks can include a change of rein at walk, organising the lesson so that they halt to have a break whilst you explain the forthcoming exercise, or ask quick quiz questions. Quiz questions

Incorrectly dressed for riding.

are particularly appropriate if you are teaching at a Pony Club centre and your riders are working towards their Achievement Badges. Very importantly, remember that children of this age become tired towards the end of each school term. Acknowledge this and adjust work accordingly, so that new topics are covered early on in the term, with repeated practice towards the end.

Children over the age of 8 or 9 are usually very active, and are often fitter to ride than many adults. They are generally co-ordinated and supple. They therefore tend to make more rapid progress than the younger pupils. However, many children aged 14–16 are focusing on important school exams and their attendance may possibly drop off a little owing to school demands. Often, for such pupils, riding is a welcome breather from studying, but stress levels may start to rise as they get close to exams.

PRIVATE LESSONS

For all ages, usually 30 minutes is a suitable length of time for an intense private lesson. Occasionally, slightly greater time is desirable, but no longer than 45 minutes. A longer time becomes too stressful for the pony as well as the rider. Semi-private lessons also tend to suit 45 minutes.

SIZE AND MIX OF CLASSES

When deciding on the size of group, there are a number of factors to consider, including experience of instructor, age and level of children, length of lesson and reliability of ponies. In every circumstance, safety is priority. An inexperienced instructor with reliable ponies and experienced children may safely teach five or six riders; a more experienced instructor should be able to control eight riders in an hour with no compromise of safety, and still deliver an interesting and challenging lesson, offering value for money.

MIXED ABILITIES OR AGES

The ideal group both for clients and instructors is one of a similar age and level of ability. This is why many centres grade their lessons, in order to assess a new rider and allocate them to the appropriate group. This way, the riders can form a cohesive group and progress together. Should one rider improve more quickly than the others, then they can move as an individual into the next level.

There are times, however, when mixed abilities are perfectly acceptable, for example, a one-off lesson for friends or relatives who would like to enjoy the experience of riding together. In this instance, at the time of booking, the riders must be informed that the lesson is always delivered at the standard of the least experienced rider.

Many centres try not to mix adults and children in lessons, however there is often a crossover with teenagers.

Mixed ages of children is inevitable, as children start riding at different ages and progress at varying rates.

Lesson planning

Every instructor should plan their lessons. The introduction of lesson planning into the Preliminary Teaching Test has helped to develop this skill early on for new instructors. The most basic lesson plan includes knowledge of the **rider's ability and goals, aim** of the lesson and therefore which **pony** is most suitable, the **location** and a basic **risk assessment**.

Rider's ability and goals will be ascertained in the first assessment lesson and updated as the rider progresses. For a beginner, the goals are set by the instructor and the rider is guided by the experience of the instructor. For a rider with some experience, the aims of lessons are formed through discussions between rider and instructor. The instructor can then guide the rider towards their aims, and reassess goals as necessary.

Aim for the lesson is dependent upon a number of factors related to goals and progress.

Selection of pony is dependent on the first two considerations, and the location in which the lesson will take place. A working knowledge of the ponies, their particular talents and behaviour for flatwork, jumping (whether showjumping or cross-country), and working indoors and outdoors (including behaviour when hacking) will help with the selection. If you are new to the riding school, freelancing, or are teaching on the child's own pony, an initial assessment of the combination in the safest environment available is essential, before aiming for specific improvement in other environments (for example, in a field, if pony and rider are not used to it).

Location is dependent on safety (see above), facilities, weather, ground conditions and goal for the lesson.

Risk assessment requires that you assess all relevant factors and decide whether there is anything else that you can do to make the lesson safer.

Internal factors include those highlighted above. To some extent, you have control of these.

A safe lesson in an indoor school.

External factors could include changing weather, livestock in a nearby field, loud noises or roadworks. You have very little control over these, but may be able to make choices to minimise or avoid their impact. For example, you plan to teach jumping in the field, with a competent child on a safe pony. You teach this combination regularly and they have been developing their jumping in the school, and you now feel that the next step is to jump outside. At the planning stage, you have minimised the risk but, on the day, roadworks are set up next to the field that you were going to use. It may be prudent to postpone the lesson to another time as the risk of an accident has become higher.

Risk assessment should continue during the lesson – fortunately, ponies and children are not robots. This adds an interesting element to teaching, but it also means that the instructor must be adaptable and not forge on blindly with their lesson plan if it requires adaptation. Part of developing as an instructor is to decide whether to continue with the same exercise, or to change it. Health and safety is top priority at all times, and decisions must be made with this in mind.

COACHING

UNDERSTANDING THE REASONS FOR RIDING

Teaching includes an understanding of basic psychology. Instructors must determine what motivates the rider. Why is the child riding? This answer gives the instructor the foundation of lesson plans, goal-setting and how to deal with problems.

Common reasons for riding:
- Love of horses and ponies.

- Aspirations to own a pony.
- Aspirations to compete.
- Aspirations to have a career with horses.
- To make friends.
- Family tradition.
- Parental pressure.

Probably the most common reason for a child to start riding, is a love of horses and ponies. Through good tuition, this passion can be nurtured.

A rider who has their sights set on owning their own pony and competing in events such as junior showjumping will be motivated and driven. They will ride regularly and have such a desire to improve that they rarely have to be told twice. These children are a joy to teach, but sometimes have such a hunger that they lack patience and can try too hard. They will be further motivated by being in a class of more able riders.

At the other extreme, a child pushed into riding by their parents may be a reluctant or even fearful pupil. Much of the instructor's role will be managing the parents with tact, to give the child and instructor enough space to progress at the right speed. In order to gain confidence, such a child will flourish if they can be placed in a class in which they are one of the stronger riders.

BEING A WIZARD INSTRUCTOR

As an instructor, you hold a highly influential position. When your pupils are younger children, trust in the instructor is often given immediately and freely. Children usually grow up in an environment where they can trust adults without question. Teenagers have a slightly different view of the world and often challenge instructors. However, they are seeking identity and require recognition and reassurance almost more than young ones.

The language that you use wields power. Be a positive wizard. Help those whom you teach to grow by using positive language to empower them. Always look on the bright side. Always finish by reminding your pupils of what they have achieved, even if it is a general statement about the group. Then talk about the next lesson, so that the positive feeling that you have just created is projected into visions of the following lesson. Pupils will then leave the lesson, looking forward to the next one; they have positive visualisation of achieving more in the next lesson. Your pupils are then more than halfway towards achieving their aim for the next lesson before they even sit on a pony! Achievement is at least 50 per cent confidence and self-belief.

The language and phrases that you use will definitely have an effect on the instructions that you give. An example of using positive language would be to say,

'Lift your hands up', rather than, 'Do not let your hands go down.' Repeated use of positive language instils a positive attitude in the rider; the reverse is applicable for the opposite. An enthusiastic instructor, who positively reinforces achievement, creates happy riders who enjoy their riding and progress to the best of their ability. Thankfully coaching has developed significantly over the past few years. There is no longer a place for the negative, barking orders type of military teaching of old.

A good instructor is reflective. At every level of qualification, we are all continually learning, and that is one aspect of teaching that is so engaging. By reflecting upon the influence that your chosen words and selection of exercises have had, you begin to build an extensive knowledge of successful vocabulary and movements. Watching other instructors teach helps develop your own skills. Listening to different explanations builds your ability to say the same thing in many different ways. An explanation that clicks with one person may need to be given in a different way to another, and this brings us on to consider learning styles.

LEARNING STYLES

We all learn in different ways. Often, we use a mixture of styles, but we usually have a dominant method of learning. When teaching riding, an instructor must be able to teach using various methods which relate to pupils' styles. In a private lesson, once the pupil's main learning style has been determined, the instructor can adapt the method, metaphor or analogy accordingly, but not to the exclusion of the other styles which may be helpful at a different time. In a group lesson, using the three main learning styles in your explanation will encompass everyone, aiding learning for all. These styles are:

VISUAL
Information is taken in by seeing what is taught, for example a picture of the digestive system; watching the reins being shortened and lengthened. Pupils using this style may need to watch the movement repeatedly.

AUDITORY
Learning from listening to information, for example, an accurate description of the aids required to bend a pony around a circle, or being told how to shorten and lengthen the reins. Pupils using this style often want to discuss what they are learning. This way, they are programming the information into their mind.

KINAESTHETIC
This involves 'feeling' and learning by performing. An example would be learning

rising trot through practice. Often, pupils using this style are keen to 'do'; to try things out. They become frustrated watching and talking about a subject, and want to have a go. Only once it has been tried can they progress, as they work out what is successful and unsuccessful. As they grasp the concept they will then need instruction to make the next step. Do not overwhelm these pupils with information. They generally respond better to being given a small instruction, trying it, then discussing it or moving on to the next step.

Understanding growth spurts

As children grow older, they develop physically, increasing in height and weight, and often this occurs in 'growth spurts'. When this happens they grow quickly over a short period of time. Sometimes, in this period, children become temporarily less co-ordinated, balanced and effective as riders. The brain takes time to adjust to new physical development. Rather than letting the child become frustrated, let them know that this is normal. As well as growing physically, the child grows mentally, developing inner strength and self-belief. School, friends and family will have great influence in this. Riding can be very effective at building self-esteem whilst retaining a humble core, but as discussed earlier, the instructor can be equally powerful negatively as positively. Careful selection of vocabulary is required, with limited criticism and maximum earned praise. No one tries to fail.

Child protection – good practice and duty of care

The British Equestrian Federation (BEF) has written a comprehensive and easily understood document: 'Child Protection Policy and Duty of Care Guidelines'. It can be downloaded from the BHS website.

Each individual instructor has their own role in child protection with the children they teach (and also in respect of vulnerable adults). Our aim when we teach is to inspire children within a safe environment, protected from harm. In this way they can develop as individuals. Through the opportunities both whilst riding and looking after ponies they can build self-esteem, take responsibility for being a member of a team, take some responsibility for the welfare of another creature, and learn to follow instructions, enjoying the feelings of satisfaction that achievement brings.

In response to the Children's Act 1989, the BEF 'fully accepts its legal and moral obligation to provide a duty of care, to protect all children (and vulnerable adults) and safeguard their welfare, irrespective of age, any disability they have, gender, racial origin, religious belief and sexual orientation.' In everyday life, the role of the instructor is to uphold this policy. First, the instructor must always exhibit exemplary behaviour as a role model for impressionable children. In front of pupils the instructor should not smoke, drink alcohol, or take drugs (which is obviously illegal anyway). You should also use appropriate language and show consideration and courtesy to others.

Poor practice, bullying and abuse are often difficult to differentiate, and it is not the instructor's responsibility to determine if abuse is occurring, but it is your responsibility to report concerns

The BEF has drafted good practice principles and it is with their kind permission that we can reproduce the following excerpt from their Child Protection Policy. Indicators of abuse or bullying include:

- Unexplained or suspicious injuries such as bruising, cuts or burns, particularly if situated on a part of the body not normally prone to such injuries.
- An injury for which the explanation seems inconsistent.
- The child describes what appears to be an abusive act involving him/her.
- Someone else (a child or adult) expresses concern about the welfare of another child.
- Unexplained changes in behaviour (e.g. becoming very quiet, withdrawn or displaying sudden outbursts of temper).
- Inappropriate sexual awareness.
- Engaging in sexually explicit behaviour.
- Distrust of adults, particularly those with whom a close relationship would normally be expected.
- Difficulty in making friends.
- Is prevented from socialising with other children.
- Displays variations in eating patterns including overeating or loss of appetite.
- Loses weight for no apparent reason.
- Becomes increasingly dirty or unkempt.

As Instructors, suspected abuse may be seen in many different environments. In each case, report your concern to a more senior person. This may be your manager at the yard where you work; it may be the organiser of a show. If there is no one senior, seek advice from the BHS, who are likely to refer you to social services. If there is abuse, you are unlikely to be the only person to have reported concerns, but it may be that your information is crucial to stopping it.

2

EARLY LESSONS – STARTING, STOPPING AND STEERING

INTRODUCTIONS, MOUNTING AND INITIAL INSTRUCTIONS

CHOOSING A SUITABLE PONY

Try to select a pony of suitable size for the rider. This can sometimes be difficult for very small children, as the most suitable lead-rein or first pony may not be the smallest. Generally, however, the instructor should be able to match up the rider to a pony of the correct size, temperament and ability. If the child is too small or too big it can compromise their position. A small rider on a large pony will find it difficult to give the leg aids, especially if their legs do not reach past the saddle flaps. Equally, a tall child on a small pony will find it hard to develop security in the lower leg with very little depth of girth beneath them.

A rider too small for the pony.

A rider too big for the pony.

PRELIMINARIES

Lessons are often considered expensive by those that take them (or pay for them). We all know there are valid reasons for the cost of lessons, but it is very important to have a professional manner and attitude in order for clients to feel that they have received value for money. Ensure that you are prepared for the lesson and that the ponies are correctly tacked and girthed up, and in the school, to guarantee that the lesson can start immediately on arrival of the children. This will relax the frequently fraught parents, and inspire confidence in the instructor. As discussed in Chapter 1, check that all riders' clothing is suitable, and that the hat of each child is of the correct standard before they mount.

THE CORRECTLY TACKED PONY

To ensure that a pony is suitably tacked up for a child's lesson the following points should apply:

Bridle – should usually be a snaffle with appropriate noseband.

Reins – check that the reins are not so long that they could hook under the child's feet when held correctly. If in doubt, tie a knot in the end of the reins to shorten them.

Neckstrap – a neckstrap should be fitted so that the rider can hold the strap comfortably for support, without having to lean forwards to reach it, or overbalance backwards.

Saddle – should be correctly fitting and well maintained, with a suitable numnah and girth. The girth should be checked before the child mounts and, if thought necessary, at some time(s) during the lesson.

A suitably tacked pony.

Stirrups – safety stirrups should be fitted for all ponies that carry children. Children's feet are often too small for adult stirrups and could potentially slip through, which could be disastrous in the event of a fall. Peacock stirrups feature an elastic side which releases when pressure is applied to it.

INTRODUCING THE CHILD TO THEIR PONY

This assumes that the child is not riding their own pony, but has come to take a lesson on a school pony. Insurance cover may be compromised if a person is inside the arena who is not part of the centre's staff. It is therefore ideal that the child is handed into your care by the parents at the entrance to the school. Also, for psychological reasons, it is advisable to focus the child on you as the instructor. This way, in their mind, you take on the role of senior adult, in the sense that you make the decisions and care for their welfare. You do not want to be in a position whereby you are asking a parent to be the 'go-between' for you and the child.

Teach the child to approach a pony correctly from the start. Lead them to the shoulder and let them say 'hello' by stroking the pony's neck. Tell them the pony's name, and reassure them that 'Smudge' has taught many children to ride, and that he really enjoys doing so. Often, young children are overwhelmed by being near such a large animal and may become very quiet. By chatting away happily, you will relax them, and often, once on board, their focus will return to you. Some other children, however, are highly enthusiastic and excited about the prospect of riding. Working with this attitude makes teaching very enjoyable, but be mindful that such children sometimes lack attention because they are too excited. For the safety of rider and pony, try to calm the child down by giving them an exercise to concentrate on, or ask them questions to gain their attention.

MOUNTING

Lead the child to the nearside, so they can mount either from a leg-up or mounting block. Make your instructions clear and concise. Once the child is mounted, check the girth and adjust the

A happy child patting the pony.

stirrup leathers. All the time, talk to the child and explain what you are doing. If you have a chatty child, ask them questions about what colour ponies they like and whether they have friends who ride.

In due course, pupils can be shown how to adjust stirrup leathers for themselves.

The experience of being on top of a pony for the first time will consume a great deal of concentration, so make instructions clear and concise. Teach the child to hold the reins correctly. Many very young children struggle at first to do this. Do not make an issue out of this, but correct gently and regularly, praising when the pupil gets it right.

The correct way to give a leg-up.

INITIAL INSTRUCTIONS

Holding the reins correctly.

Explain briefly the basic correct position – sit tall, hands up in front as if holding two glasses of water; weight down through the heels. In the early days, you may have to choose between the lower legs remaining in position and the rider's heels being down, as often the consequence of asking for 'heels down' is that the lower legs travel forwards. The depth through the heels will develop; the security in the lower legs is crucial and has far greater influence on balance and is therefore the priority.

Explain and demonstrate (auditory and visual learning styles) how to shorten and lengthen the

In due course, pupils can be shown how to adjust stirrup leathers for themselves.

A young rider demonstrating a good position.

reins correctly. Ask the child to then practise this (kinaesthetic learning style). By practising now, the child should remember later in the lesson, when you can also practise shortening and lengthening the reins. (This is also an exercise that is perfect for homework from the first couple of lessons as it can genuinely be practised at home using string, and the parents can be involved.)

Explain the basic aids to **walk**, **halt** and **turn**.

Walk – Squeeze once gently with the heels. If there is no response, use a little kick.

Halt – (First explain that 'halt' is the word we use to describe when the pony stops.) Sit tall, squeeze gently on the pony's mouth and soften the squeeze once the pony has halted.

Turn – Look in the direction of travel, open with the left hand to turn left, open with the right hand to turn right, keeping the thumb on top.

Mime as you explain how to carry out these instructions (visual and auditory learning), then actually trying it will teach kinaesthetic learners and improve co-ordination skills.

When teaching a beginner rider, keep the aids simple. Once the child can co-ordinate the rein aids, then gradually, the other aids for turning and halting can be explained – legs and upper body.

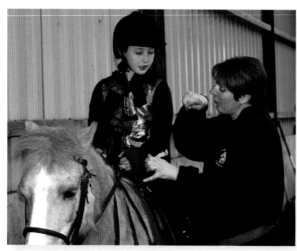

Miming to aid learning.

When you become aware of the number and complexity of instructions that we ask a young child to assimilate in a very short space of time, it becomes obvious that frequent repetition will be necessary during the first lessons. Children learn best through doing the exercise repeatedly, and success is a great motivator. If they wish to walk their pony, they will very quickly learn that a squeeze with the legs brings about the correct response. As skills become automatic and require less concentration, so the next step can be introduced. Experienced instructors can read the pupil's ability and level of learning and introduce the next step at the right time, with a valuable explanation, grasped by the pupil (checking that the pupil understands). Through correctly selected exercises, the instructor can gradually increase the challenge and thus the learning.

The first lesson

A child's first lesson should leave a happy memory that is retained forever. Centres have varying ideas of what a first lesson should consist of, and there is no one method of introducing a child to riding. The crucial aspects are that the child is safe and enjoys the experience. A 4-year-old's first lesson may include a little 15-minute 'sit on' and walk around the school (or other safe area such as a small outdoor paddock). Indeed, as our trusty school ponies sadly age and need a reduced workload, this is a good natural progression for them which keeps them working in a gentle way, From their age and experience these ponies are usually little saints, perfect for the job.

Some centres have a large waiting list for half-hour 'tiny tot' lessons, usually for children aged 4 to 6. So long as the centre has a sufficient number of experienced leaders, a small group lesson for little ones to learn in is a perfectly successful way to introduce riding, and it introduces them to new friends also. Older children may benefit from starting riding lessons on the lunge, in a manner similar to adults. The choice of method for introducing riding is dependent on the instructor's beliefs, facilities and ponies available.

Some suggestions for first lessons

VERY YOUNG CHILDREN ON THE LEAD-REIN
In many cases, children start riding on the lead-rein at 4 years old. These children are inevitably going to remain on the lead-rein for some time. Mental concentration takes time to develop, and physically they will take time to co-ordinate their aids, but as ever, safety takes priority, and before children can safely come off the lead-rein they must be able to:

- Follow instructions immediately.
- Have a correct basic, independent position.
- Understand and be able to apply the correct aids to halt, walk, trot and turn.
- Control and influence a safe pony in walk and trot.
- Maintain their distance in the ride.
- Understand the terms 'inside' and 'outside'.

OLDER CHILD IN A PRIVATE LESSON

The following ideas for initial lessons assume a child of approximately 6 years old, starting riding through private lessons.

- Go large in walk, using letters to make transitions to halt in order to practise the aids to halt and walk. Discuss how the rider communicates with the pony through the reins and legs, and how the aids should be applied. Use a gentle squeeze initially, then more firmly if there is no response. Discuss the application of the leg aid for walk– a squeeze first, followed by a nudge if there is no response.

- Use changes of rein to introduce steering and the term 'changing the rein'. Explain about inside and outside legs and hands.

- If progress is swift and the rider confident, trot can be introduced towards the end of the first lesson. This is achieved first through sitting trot, with the child holding both reins and the front of the saddle. The child should be told to relax and lean back as trot is a little bouncy, as if the pony were 'laughing'. The leader can hold both the pony and the inside ankle of the rider for security.

- To teach rising trot, start in halt at first, using a neckstrap. Explain that you are using the neckstrap to help with balance to start with, and that eventually the child will be able to rise to the trot without needing it. In halt, encourage the child to rise and sit, slowly at first, gradually increasing the 'up – down' speed until they are in the rhythm necessary for the trot of their pony. Repeat the exercise in walk, then during short periods of trot along the long sides. Once the rider begins to find the rhythm, trot can be maintained for longer periods, including through the short sides. (Be aware that the corners may initially throw the rider slightly off balance and out of rhythm.)

- The following few lessons will be a repeat of the first, gradually increasing the trot work. As the rider develops rhythm and balance, remove first the outside hand from the neckstrap. Tell the child that they can still use the neckstrap in the inside hand for balance if necessary, but that they must keep the outside hand forwards, so that they are not pulling on the pony's mouth. Once the rider can rise without balancing on the neckstrap, it can be released once in trot, and used only for the upward transition. Eventually the rider will develop balance into the transition as well.

POTENTIAL PROBLEMS IN FIRST LESSONS

NERVES

Completely understandably, children may be cautious of approaching and riding such a large animal. Every step that an instructor teaches is a foundation to build on, and therefore it should be solid. Taking time where necessary will lead to swifter progress eventually. Take the time to reassure your pupil that ponies in general are gentle giants. Teach them to respect their size and teach them how to approach safely. Take time to introduce them to the pony and teach them the significance of the pony's ears and body language, and how they can interpret how the pony feels. Given this knowledge, they will feel more confident about when it is safe to approach a pony.

Reassure the child frequently. 'This pony has taught many children to ride'; 'This pony enjoys teaching children to ride'; 'Do you see that the pony's ears are forwards? That means that he is happy to see you and would like to meet you.' All of these phrases help develop confidence.

Once the lesson has begun, most children throw caution to the wind, and are keen to progress. As an instructor, you must judge how quickly work should develop. There is a fine balance between challenging the rider and repeating the basics so that the foundation is strong.

Nerves can also be derived from the parents. For example, a nervous child may be taking their cue from a mother who wants her child to learn, but is scared of horses herself. If this is the case, chat to the mother about how talking positively, or patting the pony confidently herself will be a good example for the child.

OVERCONFIDENCE

This is as much of a problem as nerves, if not more so, and is often associated with boys more so than girls. Here, you must still spend the time repeating the basics, but make the lessons very interesting, introducing mini-challenges. For example, 'Do you think you can halt with your body exactly lined up with the marker C?' 'Let's see if you can trot for a complete circuit around the school without breaking into walk.' When such pupils want to progress to the next level, give them realistic goals to achieve in order to get there. 'When can I trot on my own?' can be answered by explaining that they must be able to achieve the requirements listed above for coming off the lead-rein.

If you are lucky enough to have a variety of facilities, ride in different areas – the school, the lungeing pen, the field, the bridleway. This keeps the initial lead-rein lessons interesting and varied.

Opening and closing gates, counting strides, working over poles (see Chapter 4) or using props all allow a lesson to be interesting whilst maintaining safety and practising exercises in a fun way. See Chapter 4 for more detail on ideas for lead-rein lessons.

SLOW PROGESS

There is no pressure of timescale that you have to work towards when teaching someone to ride. Everyone learns at different rates, and everyone will encounter problems at different times. A child who whizzes through walk and trot may struggle with the canter, at which point their peers catch up. However, as an instructor you may be put under pressure from time to time by parents, at which point you need to explain that everyone progresses at different speeds. Usually, they themselves feel under pressure from all the other parents watching the group, and are looking for an answer to go back and give them. Diplomacy is an integral part of our job. If you feel it would help, suggest some extra private lessons, just to help the child with this aspect that they find difficult. If there is homework that you can send them back with, do this. Parents can find something for the child to sit on in order to practise their 'up-downs', or provide string to practise shortening the reins.

You can also seek a second opinion. It is often fairly easy for a more senior instructor to look in unobtrusively on a lesson and offer some advice privately afterwards. In this manner, your skills develop, and rest assured, even the most experienced instructor asks for help from time to time.

Early lessons set the child up for the future. They should aim to develop initial skills, build confidence and most importantly, be enjoyable.

3

NEW WORK – MOVING ON TO TROT

WHEN AND HOW TO INTRODUCE NEW WORK

In the previous chapter, we looked at the basics of the first lessons – mounting, basic position, holding the reins, transitions between walk and halt, and basic turns. Once the child has a reasonable grasp of these basics, we can progress to something new and, logically, this will be the introduction to trot.

Before looking specifically at trot, we should consider some of the principles behind making progress in riding. Although moving on from walking to trotting is one of the early aspects of progress, understanding the criteria that determine when and whether a pupil is ready to progress is fundamental to teaching all aspects of riding.

FACTORS RELATING TO PROGRESS

How and when you introduce a new subject is dependent upon many factors including:
- The child.
- The pony.
- The facilities.
- The weather and other outside influences.
- The instructor (you and your judgement).

Let's look at these factors in more detail.

THE CHILD
Is the child introvert/extrovert, confident/nervous, younger/older, fit/unfit? Experienced instructors understand basic human and equine psychology, read body language and are able to predict how a situation is likely to unfold. As a

result, they can introduce new subjects in the way that has the greatest likelihood of success. This is what is often termed 'being a people person'. Many instructors have this quality naturally, and through experience and practice, it is refined. An unconfident or nervous child may benefit from a private lesson, where all the attention of the instructor is on them. Alternatively, they may be better in a group lesson, where they can be encouraged by their peers, and try something new after having seen others achieve it first. The parents may know which method is most likely to bring about success, and discussing the situation with them would be the starting point. Whatever the child's basic mindset, the aim is to introduce them to new things at a time when they are as receptive as possible.

A quietly confident child will be receptive to new learning and may help encourage others.

THE PONY

Every pony has his strengths, weaknesses and experience. This will influence when and how you make progress with the rider. For example, it is not uncommon to find yourself teaching a beginner child on their own pony – one whom you might consider a second pony, rather than a first pony. You are then in a position where you may feel it necessary to do more work on the lead-rein or lunge than you might with a true first pony, whilst not only teaching the rider, but also the pony. However, children often outgrow the abilities of a first pony quickly, so it is understandable why parents select a more advanced pony early on. Note, however, that progress will be hampered if a novice rider rides a green pony. This is something to be borne in mind if you have any influence over the acquisition of ponies.

However, in a riding school environment, there should be a good selection of suitably experienced ponies to work with, who can give children the correct responses to the aids – true schoolmasters. They, too, will have their strengths and weaknesses, but with a selection to choose from, the instructor can opt for the most suitable pony for particular exercises and this should assist progress.

FACILITIES

Facilities vary enormously, from a small paddock to a level indoor school with a super surface. In every aspect of teaching riding, safety takes priority. Access to good facilities will inevitably assist progress initially. An enclosed, surfaced arena with no distractions will almost certainly aid progress, but note that is does not reflect the 'real' situations that a rider may encounter later on.

When working in a field, precautions must to be taken regarding the ground conditions. For the welfare of the ponies and riders, judgements may have to be made about whether trotting is safe and, at a later stage, this will apply to a greater extent to cantering (which should not be attempted on hard or slippery surfaces). Trying to teach a child just off the lead-rein in a large field can also be a challenge, unless the pony is a saint! Safely sectioning off, a small area of the field produces an environment more conducive to a successful outcome. Moveable barriers which are helpful in this circumstance can be purchased.

THE WEATHER AND OTHER EXTERNAL INFLUENCES
The weather not only affects ground conditions if teaching in a field, but can also influence ponies in a school. Wind and rain – especially the noise of heavy rain on a school roof – may make ponies less predictable and more skittish. Hot weather saps energy (which is a safety consideration when jumping is introduced), but the heat generally relaxes ponies. Cold weather, on the other hand, tends to put ponies on their toes.

Factors such as building and maintenance work can also provide a challenge (and, if possible, should be done outside lesson hours), but sometimes the instructor has no influence over external conditions, in which case lessons must be adjusted accordingly. Either return to the lead-rein or lunge for safety, or make the work less challenging, in order to maintain safety.

THE INSTRUCTOR
We do not often think about ourselves when it comes to deciding how to introduce a new subject. We always strive to be professional, prepared and organised. Nevertheless, how we present an idea to a rider sets them up to succeed or fail, be motivated, or not. Compare these two simple introductions to trot.

'Today we are going to trot. It may be hard for you to sit to, and learning rising trot is even harder. Who would like to go first?'

'Today I am going to introduce you to one of your pony's favourite gaits, trot. It is a fun and it feels a little bouncy. As your riding improves you will find it easy to stand up and sit down whilst your pony trots, which we call rising trot.'

Compare the two pictures that form in your mind from these very different descriptions of the same activity. The first sets up a negative attitude to experiencing trot for the first time, which will inevitably make it more difficult than it need be. The second gives ownership of the pony to the child, whether he is theirs or not, and then tells the child that the pony enjoys trot – a positive image. The description then imbues the child with a sense of fun, saying it may feel bouncy. (Describe trot as 'slow and gentle' for children who are very nervous.) Then the child is told that it will be easy to learn rising trot, with practice.

The sub-conscious is a tool for the conscious. If you tell the sub-conscious that something is easy, the conscious finds it easier than had you been negative, so be positive in your choice of words. 'Keep your heels down' is far more positive than 'Don't let your heels come up.'

MOVING ON TO TROT
FIRST STEPS

A smiling, enthusiastic instructor will help instil confidence in pupils starting new work.

As explained previously in this chapter, teaching is an art and, as such, has no set formula. There is thus no set period of time to walk, before trot can be introduced. However, the child should be confident, and able to understand how to halt, walk and steer before trot work begins.

These skills should be practised on the lead-rein. This may take 15 minutes, 25 minutes or a number of lessons. If the child has been introduced to riding before and has had a bad first experience of trotting, the time taken before trotting again may be longer whilst confidence is restored.

Introduce the pupil to sitting trot initially, and create a gentle, slow trot down the long side. Most children will be giggling by the end of it. Teach them to hold on to the front of the saddle as well as the reins, and to lean back slightly and relax. Once they have relaxed and gained a feel for the movement, then teach rising trot.

The tack that the child holds for balance when learning to trot is up to personal preference. I prefer a well-fitted neckstrap because then the position of the rider's hands allows the freedom to stand up and sit down, whereas I find that holding the pommel of the saddle puts the hands into the wrong position and tends to make the rider lean back too far, causing insecurity in the lower leg. Practise rising at halt, walk and then introduce it at trot. Short periods of rising trot prevent the child from becoming tired. This also allows the instructor the opportunity to give minor corrections frequently, setting a small goal for the next trot. Begin trot work in a straight line as this will aid balance, then introduce trotting around a corner, where the rider learns to balance on a curve. Intersperse the trot with periods of walk, repeating transitions and steering in inventive ways.

Sitting trot for the first time.

If you are not leading yourself, remember the helper who is, and don't wear them out! Also consider the temperature, and in the hotter months do not allow leaders, ponies or children to become overheated. (Chapter 4 discusses how to train leaders.)

As the child gains balance and rhythm, so they will require the neckstrap less and less. Before trying without it, ask the child to push their hands forwards slightly, releasing the pressure on the neckstrap. This way, if they have a wobble, they regain balance by using the neckstrap, rather than pulling on the pony's mouth.

Practising rising at halt.

Teach the child to release the outside hand from the neckstrap first, that is, to carry the outside rein whilst trotting with the neckstrap in the inside hand. The next step is to release the neckstrap completely. Continue to use the neckstrap for the transition into trot for a short time.

Once the child is trotting without the neckstrap, the next difficulty may be ensuring that the reins do not slip through

A young beginner rising with only the inside hand on the neckstrap.

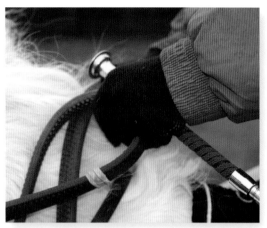

Using a marker to assist holding the reins correctly.

their fingers. One method of resolving this problem is to place an elastic band as a marker around the reins where they need to be held. The pupil then begins to gain a feel for the length of reins required and the gentle, consistent pressure on the pony's mouth.

RECOGNISING SIGNS OF FATIGUE

No one, whether child or adult, is going to learn new work effectively when they are tired, so it is up to the instructor in all situations to recognise signs of fatigue.

As a guide, 30 minutes is a sufficient length of time for a private lesson for a beginner of any age, using a mixture of walk and trot.

Children often have a natural level of fitness that adults often do not possess. However those of just 4-6 years olds are very young and do not have high levels of sustainable energy. Strength and stamina tend to build from 6 years onwards, through all the activities children do.

Obvious signs of fatigue, which should not be ignored, are:

- Red face.
- Loss of position/collapsing in the position.
- Increased respiration rate.
- Request to change the exercise to walk.
- Request to finish the lesson.
- Saying 'I'm tired'.

Signs of fatigue should not be ignored.

4

LEAD-REIN LESSONS

The child rider is on the lead-rein for a relatively short period of time during their riding career. The length of time will vary according to many factors, including frequency of lessons, age, physical development, desire to ride and learning ability.

UNDERLYING AIMS

There are several aims that should be at the back of the instructor's mind whilst teaching lead-rein lessons.

An enjoyable introduction to riding on the lead-rein will help to produce happy, confident riders such as those pictured here.

DEVELOPING CONFIDENCE AND ATTENTION
CONFIDENCE

Lead-rein lessons are the first steps on a path that hopefully, at the very least, will be an enjoyable hobby for the rest of the rider's life. Experiences in the beginning need to be positive to promote confidence. To a great extent, the instructor is in control of the child achieving this. The instructor has control of the pony, and the instructor has the ability to praise the child, guide them through their first learning experiences and give interesting lead-rein lessons that are fun, thus establishing trust between instructor and pupil.

FOLLOWING INSTRUCTIONS

Older children are generally used to following instructions, having been at school. This is not always the case for 4- and 5-year-olds, and one of the reasons why parents may encourage their children to ride is the benefit of learning how to listen, understand and follow instructions. Everyone learns through a different style or mixture of styles (see Chapter 1) and part of the instructor's job is to discover how best to explain to the rider what is required. The best instructors do this instinctively and are a pleasure to watch, as they help the rider to understand and prevent frustration. If the child fails to do the task that you have set, look first to the method that you have used to explain the concept and describe it in a different way.

DEVELOPING TECHNIQUE
PRACTISING STARTING, STOPPING AND STEERING

Learning to steer on the lead-rein.

The aims of lead-rein lessons are to introduce the child to ponies, and to begin work on creating a solid foundation for riding. This requires the child to be taught correctly from the start. Exercises can give correct information and still be fun. In order to prepare children to come off the lead-rein, they must be taught to apply the correct and effective aids to halt, walk, trot and turn. These skills will take much practice and will form the fundamental basis of each lesson, no matter what the particular focus of an individual exercise may be.

Shortening and lengthening the reins is a basic skill required from all riders. For many young children it is actually one of the harder early skills to master, and will require much prompting and repeated demonstration to develop. As mentioned earlier it is, however, a task that can be set as homework, as it does not require a pony, and can be practised with a piece of string. Show the parents – adults will pick it up immediately.

Shortening the reins.

LEARNING ABOUT INSIDE AND OUTSIDE

Unfortunately, we sometimes find ourselves teaching a piece of information, only to have to change it years later. 'Inside' and 'outside' fall into this category. These terms really refer to the pony's bend, however for simplicity when we teach a young child, we use it in reference to the school. The inside leg, hand and rein are those closer to the centre of the school, whilst the outside leg, hand and rein are nearer the outside of the school. 'Simon says' is the best game to play in order to learn about inside and outside with a little fun. For example, 'Simon says put both reins into the outside hand, and touch your head with your inside hand.' (In this game, if you give an instruction without the prefix 'Simon says', and the rider completes the instruction, they are 'out'.)

PRACTISING THE CORRECT BASIC POSITION

Using the song, 'Head, shoulders, knees and toes', children can substitute those words for 'Ear, shoulder, hip and heel' to learn the points that should be in a straight vertical line when in the correct position for flatwork.

As instructors, we should always have an image in our minds of 'best practice' when teaching. This is a mental image that we use to compare what we are seeing in front of us, with the ideal. There will rarely be 'perfection' (how many times does a '10' appear on a dressage score sheet?) but the image helps us to train riders by analysing the differences between the compared pictures.

Children are in the process of learning to co-ordinate their aids, and any change will be gradual, and will need repeated encouragement. Give one primary positional correction, rather than many, as the pupil is more likely to remember one. Try to choose the correction that is at the core of the problems, as this may have the effect of correcting the others.

A good position from the rider – and the pony in a square halt.

Leading a pony safely.

LEARNING ABOUT BASIC EQUINE PSYCHOLOGY AND SAFE HANDLING

Children generally (and hopefully) start riding from an interest in or love of horses. This love for the animal can be nurtured by the instructor. Learning to ride should not be just about riding the pony. Good practice when handling, approaching and walking around ponies must be taught from the outset. This is one of the duties of care that you accept as an instructor and is very much our responsibility. Basic horse psychology develops an understanding of equine motivation, such as herd instinct, and helps to expand the rider's appreciation of the pony as a sentient creature and partner. It can be incorporated into every lesson in a very informal way: repetition is absolutely necessary for good habits to develop.

LESSON PROPS AND LEADERS

PROPS

Props make lessons more interesting. They also help to focus the rider and, a little like jumping a fence where you either clear it, or have four faults, children can see for themselves whether they have achieved the exercise rather than it being subject to the instructor's decision. Exercises using props can therefore be both self-motivating and rewarding.

Suggested equipment:
- Cones – there are a variety available, from traffic cones to training cones used for rugby or football.
- Poles – an instructor will find many uses for a ground-pole to help explain a concept.
- Mounted games equipment – flags, bending poles, buckets and sponges.

Leaders

Riding schools often run smoothly at the weekend through the aid of 'helpers'. Helpers will often be 'leaders' for lead-rein lessons and are a valuable asset to every instructor so long as the instructor provides sufficient, correct and thorough training. Often, riding schools set minimum age limits for helpers and certainly as an instructor you want level-headed leaders with common sense and the ability to follow instructions. For a lead-rein lesson, it is ideal to have a headcollar underneath the pony's bridle to which a lead-rope can be attached. This gives control to the leader without unnecessary interference with the pony when the leader runs alongside.

Best practice would probably suggest that leaders should wear hat and gloves to lead, along with the usual riding clothes. Each establishment will make their own decisions based upon their own risk assessments, as there are no rules governing this.

Through training, the leader learns to help the rider whenever necessary with the exercise given by the instructor. A well-trained leader will be ultimately in control of the speed and location of the pony (distance from pony in front) in the ride, and will focus on instructions from the instructor, helping the rider when necessary. Often, through lack of training, the leader ignores the rider, and simply controls the pony. The leader must understand that an awareness of the rider is imperative at all times for safety, but also to assist the child to follow instructions. Ensure that your leaders introduce themselves to their children, but that they do not chat continually during the lesson, instead allowing the riders to focus on the instructor. Good practice always keeps the leader on the inside of the pony, so that the leader is not squashed between the pony and the wall of the school, and they should lead from the pony's shoulder.

The instructor should help to develop leaders' skills in various ways. For example, teach them always to ask the child first if they need to hold their leg whilst trotting, or whether they need to change length of stirrup leathers.

Lead-rein lesson plans

The following lesson plans are adaptable for either private, semi-private or group lessons and are designed for lessons of approximately 30 minutes. During a group lesson, riders will not be able to repeat the exercise as many times as an individual in a private lesson.

In order to develop the rider's skills, and also to maintain interest and offer a focus, the lesson plans offer ideas to use as themes in the lessons. Each lesson should begin with a warm-up of walk, trot and changes of rein which is a recap and practice of basic skills.

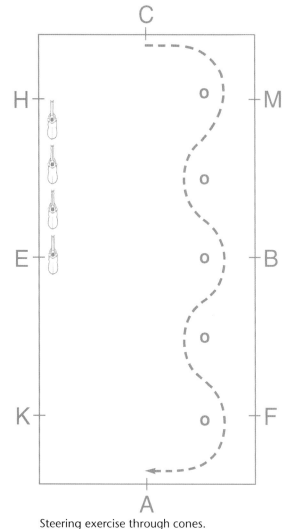

Steering exercise through cones.

STEERING

- Using five cones, position them, evenly spaced, along the three-quarter line on one side of the school.
- Start in walk to help each child with their steering, explaining how to open the rein to turn. Ask riders to imagine carrying a glass of water in each hand in order to maintain the position of the hands on the reins. The aim is not to spill any water!
- Try this in trot. Even riders who hold their neckstrap can achieve this exercise. Show them how to steer by swapping their neckstrap from hand to hand as they weave through the cones.
- For more advanced lead-rein riders, this exercise can be turned into a game. In a private lesson you can time the rider through the cones, adding seconds for any missed. In a group you could do the same, or have two sets of cones for races.
- This exercise helps develop the ability to follow instructions, steering and co-ordinating the aids.

SIGNALLING

- Set up poles in a cross shape.
- Teach the riders how to signal left and right, as you would in Riding and Road Safety training. Explain why signals must be very clear and why they must look before they signal.
- Use the cross to practise signalling. Ensure that riders have enough time to look and signal before they reach the junction.
- When this exercise becomes familiar, and you have a good group of lead-rein riders, you can set it up so that it is a miniature course for them to ride around, incorporating a little trot.
- As each 'turn' can be time-consuming, this is an exercise very suited to private lessons. Alternatively, you can have a couple of riders on the 'course' at any one time. Your leaders should be sufficiently experienced to help the children, as you will not be able to give all your attention to each individual.

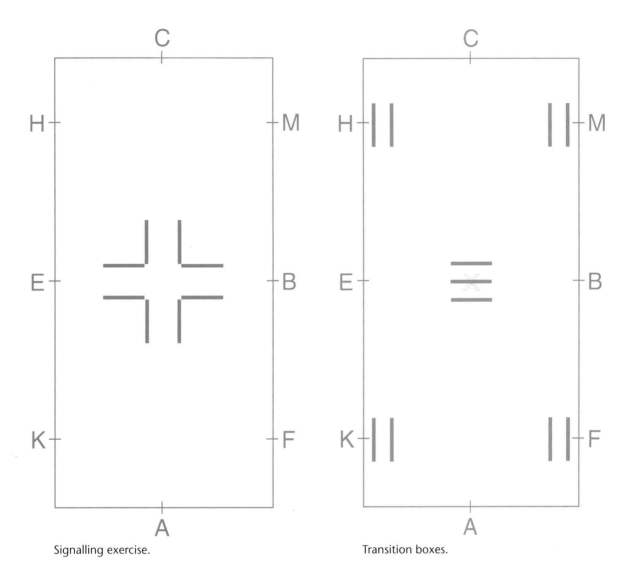

Signalling exercise.

Transition boxes.

- Much of the time is spent in walk and the exercise is therefore suited to the summer so the children do not become cold (as they might in winter), and to the end of school term when the children may be tired. This teaches them very valuable road-craft skills and is also valuable for practising transitions between walk and halt, and being able to make precise turns.

TRANSITIONS

- Use poles to set up 'transition boxes' at various points around the school. These 'boxes' are simply two poles, one on either side of the track. If you are primarily working the ride going large, these could be at K,H, M and F. If you are working on two 20m circles, they could be at A, X and C. These 'boxes' offer a more tangible place to make a transition than just a letter. For example, you can insist that the rider halts the pony with his legs between the poles. This also gives the rider the awareness of where the hind legs are.

- Recap the aids for halt, walk and trot, including how to begin with a light aid, and gradually increasing the pressure.
- Begin with transitions from walk to halt in the boxes, counting the halt for a certain number of seconds. Then make the transition to walk. Repeat in as many boxes as you have set up.
- Develop the exercise to include walk and trot transitions, walking in one box, and trotting in the next.
- This exercise emphasises the application of the aids and develops confidence in the rider's ability to control the pony.

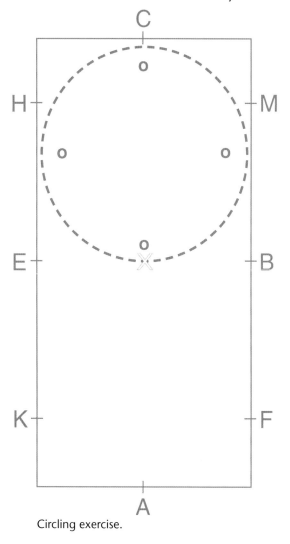

Circling exercise.

CIRCLING

- Placing 'black dots' on the wall of the school to identify where the circle leaves and rejoins the track on 20m circles at A and C is invaluable when teaching circles at any level. For the child on the lead-rein, also position cones at the letter (for example A), both black dots and X. this gives the rider something physical to aim for.
- Teach the riders to walk around the 20m circle, training them to look a quarter of a circle ahead all the time.
- Progress the exercise to trot.
- During a group lesson, have the whole ride in walk on the circle, trotting one at a time to the rear of the ride, then two at a time, eventually building up to the whole ride trotting together on the circle.
- This exercise teaches spatial awareness and introduces a very important school figure.

CHANGING THE LENGTH OF STRIDE

- Varying the length of stride comes with the ability to apply the aids so that the stride length varies but the rhythm remains constant.

A lead-rein rider does not have this ability, but they can be taught that they can vary the pony's stride, even though the rhythm does change.

- In walk, ask the rider to try to take tiny, baby steps, then to ask for large, giant steps. Explain that they are going to use the reins to slow the pony down to make the stride smaller, and ask the question, 'If you just use the reins, what might happen?' They will reply that the pony may stop, at which point you can ask them how they could prevent that from happening. The answer will come that they must use their legs. The same question can be posed when you talk about trot – baby steps and giant steps.
- A useful trot exercise is to ride small steps down one long side and giant steps along the opposite long side. Count the number of steps on both long sides to compare the difference.
- This is the first exercise that teaches the rider to co-ordinate their aids, that is, legs and hands together. It is another exercise that is self-teaching. For example, if the rider fails to use legs as well as hands to create small steps in trot, the pony will walk. Equally, the rider appreciates their results when they apply the aids correctly.

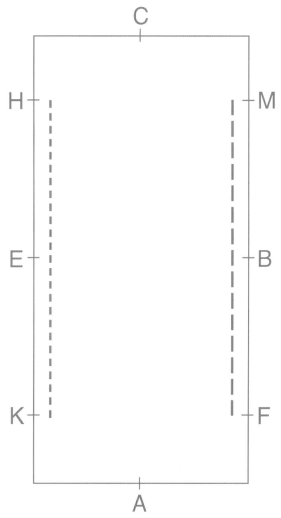

Exercise in changing stride length.

RIDING WITHOUT STIRRUPS

- Introducing work without stirrups to lead-rein riders creates a positive early basic experience.
- As with all these topics, the aim is to give the child a positive experience to set them up for following work.
- Always underestimate how quickly to progress during early lessons in order to build confidence, rather than creating a challenge that is too large.
- Removing stirrups for the first time can be achieved at halt. Teach riders how to cross their stirrups over and then introduce leg exercises. These can include: Scissors – the rider gently swings one leg forward whilst the other leg travels back; Jockey – each knee in turn is brought up to the front of the saddle, like a

Working without stirrups.

jockey, and then moved away from the saddle, and gently pushed back and down.

■ The next time, get the riders to quit their stirrups in halt. Then perform the exercises in walk.

■ By the next time you choose to develop the work without stirrups, the riders should be confident enough to try a little trot without stirrups. Train the leaders to hold their rider's inside ankle and only trot down the long side to begin with. (A leader's inclination will be to pull down on the inside ankle to hold the child in position. Explain that this will actually pull the rider to the side, unbalancing them, and that the aim is to maintain stability and leg position, therefore the leader should help to hold the leg in position.) Repeat until the rider no longer needs the support of the leader, and extend the trot to include corners – watch out for wobbles as riders trot around corners at first.

■ Working without stirrups, introduced correctly, increases balance and confidence and develops the position.

RIDING WITHOUT REINS

■ Working without reins is a liberating exercise, and often produces surprise results. A rider who has struggled to rise to the trot without the neckstrap is suddenly able to rise and windmill their arms at the same time! The reason for this is that the focus has been taken away from the rising, allowing it to happen more automatically.

■ With the rest of the group in halt, one rider at a time can perform exercises along one long side. The leader has complete control of the pony.

■ Tie a knot in the reins and, in walk, perform exercises with the rider's upper body. Exercises include backward windmills, which help the rider to sit tall and straight, arms to the side, twisting from the waist with arms outstretched to the side, which helps suppleness in the back, and standing up with arms out straight in front, which aids balance.

Working without reins.

- Each of these exercises can eventually be performed in trot.
- Try singing the rhyme, 'Head, shoulders, knees and toes.' The rider can complete the actions to the song, but only in walk!
- Try playing 'Simon says'.
- These exercises help develop balance, co-ordination and confidence.

JUMPING POSITION

- Children are ever so accepting of new ideas. Introducing jumping position at this early stage builds a foundation for jumping later on.
- Lead-rein stirrup leathers are often short enough not to require adjustment for jumping position. However, do adjust if necessary.
- Tell the rider to put the stirrups on the balls of their feet, with their heels down, as normal. As well as holding the reins, grasp a piece of mane just in front of the saddle. Instruct them to push their seat to the rear of saddle, lean forwards and lift up so that they are hovering over the saddle.
- Practise this in halt and walk and, before trying it in trot, ask the rider to practise bouncing on their knees – a necessary skill to absorb the movement in trot. Explain that they do not need to rise to the trot when in jumping position.
- Practise short periods of trot in a balanced position. As the child becomes competent in rising trot, alternate in trot between rising and jumping position.

Introducing jumping position on the lead-rein.

EARLY POLE-WORK

■ To develop the jumping position further, add work over trotting-poles. One individual pole initially is sufficient challenge for a lead-rein rider to aim for the centre, take jumping position over the pole, return to rising trot and steer around the next corner. All effort will need to be supported by the leader, at least initially.

■ To help achieve the correct turn, position cones for the rider to turn through on to the correct line, and to maintain a straight line away from the pole.

■ The exercise can develop in the next lesson to link two poles together, on diagonal lines.

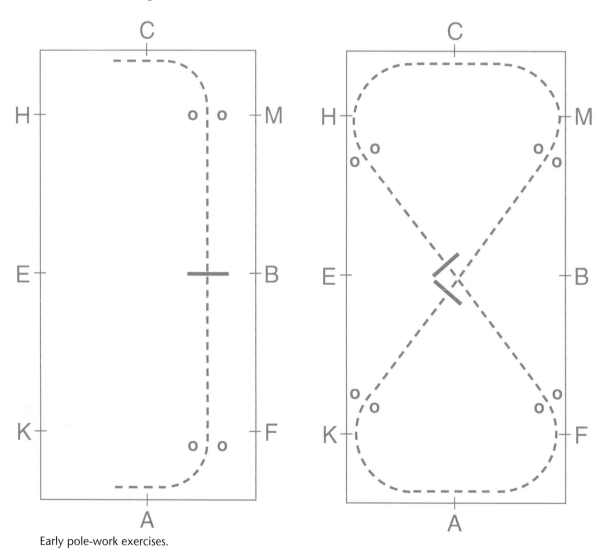

Early pole-work exercises.

5

MOUNTED GAMES

Children learn through explanation, trial and error, and experimenting. They learn quickly if the exercise is fun and they learn quickly if the exercise is rewarding. Mounted games cover all of these bases.

Towards the end of the school term, when children can become tired, games can be an enjoyable way of testing all the skills that they have been taught. They can also be used as a treat at the end of a particularly good lesson when the riders deserve a reward.

Children are naturally competitive. As an instructor, you have to be careful that you choose exercises that cover different aspects of riding so that everyone has the opportunity to excel. If you have a very talented rider who wins everything, either move them up into the next group, or handicap them somehow, for example by getting them to perform the same game as the others, but without stirrups, or to ride a more challenging pony. In reality, we often have to manage groups of varying ability, and we learn to put everyone on the same level in order to be as fair as possible. Safety always comes first.

The mounted games described in this chapter cover a wide spectrum of abilities, from lead-rein games to Pony Club Championship games. (A comprehensive list of Junior Games can be found on the Pony Club website: www.pcuk.org)

Obviously, it is necessary to stick to the more basic games in the earlier stages of riders' development. However, in addition to selecting the correct games for each ability, you have the option of making the game easier or harder depending upon which gait it is ridden in.

EQUIPMENT

Here is a list of equipment that is required for the mounted games in this chapter.
- Potatoes and spoons
- Cones
- Tennis balls
- Sturdy buckets

- Grooming kit box and safe, soft grooming kit items
- Old socks
- Rope
- Flags
- Litter bin (large)
- Sacks
- Quoits

BASIC GAMES

'SIMON SAYS'

This game has been mentioned in previous chapters. Whilst the riders are in walk, trot or canter, give instructions with the prefix 'Simon says', for example, 'Simon says, putting both reins in the outside hand, place your inside hand on your head.' If you give an instruction without the prefix, and the rider completes the instruction, they are 'out'.

This game teaches lead-rein riders to listen to the instruction carefully, and reinforces knowledge of inside and outside. For older children it helps them to concentrate on more than one task at a time, for example, trotting or cantering and following the instructor's commands.

COLOURS

With the ride spread out around the school or field, call the colours. These colours can be given different meanings, for example:

Orange = stop

Pink = walk

Green = trot

If you have older, competent children, you could include:

Red = canter

Purple = turn a small circle

After a couple of practice runs, the last rider to make the transition is 'out' and comes to stand in the middle of the school. Give penalties for riders who ride the transitions badly: you want to try to avoid the riders pulling madly on the reins to stop first! For example, give each rider two 'lives'. They lose a life for each badly ridden transition, and are automatically 'out' when they lose their two lives. The instructor needs to choose a good vantage point in order to be able to have a good view of all of the riders.

Letter game

Using the letters around the school, allocate each child a letter. Depending on their ability, they must walk, trot or canter to the letter and then halt next to it with their hand touching the letters. It does not count if they touch it as their pony walks past. If this happens they must come around again and halt next to it.

To prevent crashes in the school, insist that they stick to the track and give each rider a letter that is a few letters ahead of where they are.

Obstacle course

An obstacle course can be made as hard or easy as you like, not only from the elements included, but also the gait/speed at which it is ridden. If you are teaching a group, you can either divide them into teams and run it like a race, or you can time each individual as they ride around the course. Think of, and explain the penalties for each error before they occur, especially if you have weighted the penalties in any way. For example, 4 seconds added if you miss out a bending cone.

Touching letters.

Possible elements to include are:
- Bending
- Pick up and drop/place
- Ride and lead
- Stepping stones
- A small fence
- Transitions
- Round the world (for lead-rein riders only, otherwise it gets too fast and dangerous!)

An example of how a course could be set up is shown in the drawing overpage.

Pony Club mounted games

The following is a selection of official Pony Club (PC) mounted games, from the Senior Area Games of 2009, reproduced with kind permission. This book aims

Example of a simple obstacle course.

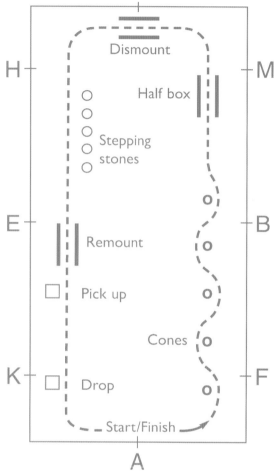

H

E

K

M

B

F

A

Dismount

Half box

Stepping
stones

Remount

Pick up

Cones

Drop

Start/Finish

Part of an obstacle course.

to cover the basics of teaching children to ride, from riding schools to Pony Club, from freelance in a field to warming up for Pony Club Championships. The Pony Club is a highly valuable society through which many great riders have first developed their riding skills and shown competitive potential. Mounted games are not only great fun for pony and rider; they develop team spirit and camaraderie and can be astonishing to watch.

Specialist equipment, as used in some more advanced games, can be costly to purchase and many centres gradually build up a collection of items. However, you can always find cheap alternatives, such as traffic cones rather than purpose-made bending poles.

Event 1 – Bending

Lines of five bending poles will be erected from 7–9m apart. On the signal to start, Number One, carrying a baton, rides down and back through the bending poles. On returning to and crossing the start line he hands the baton to Number Two. Numbers Two, Three and Four will similarly ride down and back through the bending poles in succession.

The winning team will be the one whose Number Four is first past the finish line, mounted, and carrying the baton.

Knocked down poles must be replaced by the rider concerned.

Line Stewards will not signal unless the bending pole is broken or lying flat on the ground.

Event 2 – Ball and cone

There will be two cones for each team, placed level with the 1st and 4th bending poles. A tennis ball is placed on the far cone. Numbers One and Three will be mounted behind the start line and Numbers Two and Four behind the changeover line. Number One carries a tennis ball, and on the signal to start, rides to the first cone and places his ball on it. He then rides to the second cone, collects the ball and hands it to Number Two. Numbers Two, Three and Four complete the course in a similar manner. The winning team is the one whose Number Four is first over the finish line carrying the ball.

In the case of cones knocked over or a ball being dropped, General Rules apply.

Event 3 – Stepping stones

Six stepping stones for each team will be placed across the centre line about 30cm apart and in a straight line up and down the arena between the lines of bending poles.

Numbers One and Three will be mounted at the start/finish end of the arena and Numbers Two and Four at the changeover end.

On the signal to start, Number One rides to the stepping stones, dismounts and, leading his pony, steps on each stone and then the ground before remounting to cross the line.

Number Two, Three and Four will similarly complete the course up or down the arena in succession.

Should any pony or rider knock over a stepping stone, or should a rider step on the ground crossing the stones, he must set up the fallen stones and in both cases return to cross all the stones again – even if it is the last one which has fallen.

Riders must lead the pony by the rein nearer to them.

Event 4 – Tack shop

A bending pole topped with a 'money box' will be erected level with the first bending post. A plastic grooming tray will be placed upon an upturned litter bin level with the fourth bending pole.

The Number Five stands behind a table or upturned litter bin placed 3m behind the changeover line. On this table will be four items (a dandy brush, tin of metal polish, tail bandage and a tin of saddle soap).

Number One will carry a 'coin'. On the signal to start, Number One rides and places the coin in the 'money box', continues to collect the grooming tray and then rides to Number Five, who puts any one of the items in the grooming tray. Number One then returns the tray to the first table. He then rides to the 'money box' collects the 'coin' and hands it to Number Two behind the start line.

Numbers Two, Three and Four will complete the course in the same way.

The winning team will be the one whose Number Four is first over the finishing line carrying the 'coin'.

If an item is dropped behind the changeover line, either the rider or Number Five may pick it up. The item must be in the tray before the rider re-crosses the changeover line. The Number Five may hold the rein of the pony behind the changeover line.

EVENT 5 – OLD SOCK

3m behind the changeover line, each team will have four socks sewn into balls about the size of a fist, within a ring marked on the ground (for visibility). Across the centre will be a row of buckets, one for each team.

All four riders form up behind the start/finish line. On the signal to start, Number One, carrying a sock, rides to his team's bucket and drops the sock into it. He rides to the far end, dismounts, picks up a sock, remounts and returns to the start to hand it to Number Two.

Numbers Two, Three and Four will complete the course in the same way in succession, with Number Four dropping the last sock into the bucket on his way back.

The winning team will be the one whose Number Four is first over the finish line.

Socks knocked out of the circle should be replaced by the Line Steward concerned.

EVENT 6 – ROPE

Lines of four bending posts will be erected approx 7–9m apart.

Numbers One and Three will be behind the start/finish line and Numbers Two and Four behind the changeover line. Number One will carry a rope (the rope must not be looped or knotted).

On the signal to start, Number One will ride up through the bending poles to cross the changeover line, where Number Two will grasp the rope and both riders return through the bending posts to the start line.

On crossing the line, Number One will release the rope and Number Three will grasp it. Numbers Two and Three, each holding the rope, then ride up through the bending posts to cross the changeover line, where Number Two will release the rope and Number Four will grasp it. Numbers Three and Four then return back through the bending poles to the finish, each holding the rope.

EVENT 7 – TWO MUGS

On a line of four bending poles, a mug is placed on each of the 1st and 3rd poles. Numbers One and Three form up on the start line, Numbers Two and Four on the changeover line.

On the signal to start, Number One moves the mug from pole 1 to pole 2, the mug from pole 3 to pole 4 and then rides across the changeover line. Number Two moves the mugs from pole 4 to 3 and pole 2 to pole 1 respectively and then crosses the start/ finish line.

Number Three repeats the actions of Number One, and Number Four repeats the actions of Number Two.

Event 8 – Five flags

A flag holder will be placed 3m behind the changeover line and another on the centre line. Each team will have five flags on canes. Four of these will be in the team's holder on the centre line and one will be carried by Number One at the start.

On the signal to start, Number One rides to the other end of the arena and places the flag he is carrying in the flag holder. He rides back, picks a flag out of his team's holder on the centre line and hands this flag to Number Two behind the start line.

Numbers Two, Three and Four will complete the course in the same way up and down the arena in succession so that, at the end, the team will have placed four flags in the holder at the far end of the arena and Number Four finishes over the start line mounted and carrying the fifth flag.

Should the flag holder be knocked over, the rider must put it up again, replacing any flags there may have been in it. Should a rider take more than one flag from the holder, he must replace the surplus. He may dismount to correct mistakes.

If a flag should come off the cane, the stick may be used to complete the race.

On windy days rubber bands can be used to keep the flags furled and prevent them blowing together.

Early gymkhana games can be fun, and a springboard for more advanced games and activities.

6

INTRODUCING CANTER

The introduction of canter work is a red-letter period in anyone's riding career. Children have a mixture of reactions to canter. Some will be ever so keen to try. Maybe they have friends who ride at a higher level, and they wish to be doing the same as them, or perhaps they are confident children who are enthusiastic to progress. Others may be less positive in their approach. It is important not to push children to canter before they are ready. By explaining that they are ready to canter, but making the decision theirs, when they do say yes, they approach canter in a more positive frame of mind. This is more likely to lead to a positive outcome.

When you are in a situation where you are teaching a nervous rider in a private lesson, it may be of benefit to put them into a group of the same level for a short period. In this way, they see other children learning to canter and this often motivates them to try. At the very least, watching others learning to canter will illustrate the process.

WHEN TO INTRODUCE CANTER

The decision to introduce canter is the instructor's. As you gain experience in teaching, you will begin to see the ingredients necessary for a successful outcome. Until this point, ask a more senior instructor to watch the child ride, and gain experience from listening to what they say. Try not to be swayed by the child or their parents. The child may be very confident, but that can be lost in an instant from a fall during their first canter. Parents often have little equestrian knowledge and simply want to see their child progress. You must be almost 100 per cent certain that the first few experiences are going to be constructive in order to create a positive foundation.

You want to be sure that:
- You have selected the right pony (see below).
- The pony is competent in canter (especially if the child is riding their own pony and you have not seen him canter).
- The weather conditions are right and ground conditions are good if you are in a small enclosed field.

- You choose the right time of year. Introduce canter. if possible, in the summer when ponies tend to live out, and the sunshine relaxes them. If the ponies live in over the winter, they may have too much excess energy for introducing canter to a novice rider.
- The child is confident and enthusiastic to learn to canter
- The child has a basically correct, secure position. (Often time spent in jumping position helps to develop greater security in the lower leg, and is therefore valuable to introduce before canter.)
- You can work in an enclosed, safe area with no distractions.

Choosing the right pony

Choosing the right pony for the rider to learn canter on is crucial. Having a choice available is one of the great advantages for both pupil and instructor in a riding school.

A pony who can safely teach a rider to canter has many qualities, including:

- Experience – usually this comes with age.
- Safety – this also often develops with age.
- A basic willingness to canter.
- A balanced canter.
- A steady canter.
- A comfortable canter.
- Responsiveness and obedience to the instructor and rider.

A reliable mount is needed for introducing canter.

Usually, riding schools have a good selection of ponies, each with different qualities. There should be at least a couple who excel at teaching children to canter, are unflappable even if the child bounces a little, and stoically accept their cantering responsibility.

HOW TO INTRODUCE CANTER

There are many different scenarios to introducing canter, as it may be in a group or private lesson, on a riding school pony or the child's own, in an arena or small, enclosed field. The crucial factors are to ensure that you think that the child and pony are ready and that you have prepared the lesson to be as safe as possible. We must be adaptable and if, on the days you have planned to introduce canter, external influences compromise the safety, leave it for another day.

Practising sitting trot is a must before canter. The child should have worked regularly without stirrups before cantering, and preferably have practised sitting trot with stirrups also, as this is sometimes harder initially.

There are a variety of methods for introducing canter:

- On the lunge – a reliable pony on the lunge, with a steady, comfortable canter, would be the ideal scenario for teaching canter.
- In a private lesson at a riding school – using a reliable pony who responds to the instructor's commands for a short canter. The number of canter strides can gradually be increased.
- If you are teaching a child on their own pony, you need to see how the pony reacts in the canter before you set about teaching your novice rider. The family may have an older sibling who can demonstrate the canter first, but remember that an experienced rider will ride differently from the novice. If the pony lunges well, you may be able to introduce canter on the lunge, otherwise use an enclosed area that the pony is familiar with, and I personally would run beside the pony and child at first, with the pony on a lead-rein. Gradually you can assess the rider and pony and gauge how both are feeling, and develop from there, needing to run less and less.
- In a group lesson at a riding school – ensure that each child knows that they can canter when they are ready, and that just because it is being introduced into the group lesson, they do not have to try straight away. With the ride in halt, one rider at a time, make transitions through walk to trot, and make the canter transition in the allocated corner. Continue the canter for a few strides along the long side, returning to rising trot afterwards. You can send an older, fast-running leader if you do not have sufficient control of the pony in canter from your voice. Teach your most confident child first, who is then likely to give the others confidence through achieving the exercise.

Teaching the Aids for Canter

Teaching a rider the aids for canter is built up in layers.

1 An older child can learn the three-beat sequence of footfalls in the canter early on. During left canter, this is right hind, left hind and right fore together, followed by the left fore, also known as the 'leading leg'. The opposite is true for right-lead canter.

2 In an ideal situation the rider does not 'ask' for canter at first. Instead, the instructor should have control of the transition. This allows the rider to concentrate on position. The instructor should tell the rider to relax and lean back slightly, with relaxed legs, wrapped around the pony's sides. In addition to holding the reins (without pulling back on them), the rider's fingers should be tucked under the pommel; this will help pull the rider gently deeper into the saddle. The instructor should encourage the rider to relax with the movement of the canter. Often, inexperienced riders find the canter very bouncy until they learn to sit into it. The following are some analogies that may help the rider to sit deeper in the saddle.

   ■ Ask the rider to imagine that they are on a swing, and that for each beat of the canter, they move their seat in the same way that they would on the forward arc of the swing.
   ■ Tell the rider to 'polish the saddle with their seat'.
   ■ Tell the rider to 'glue their seat to the saddle'.
   ■ Ask the rider to wrap their legs around the pony's sides, and to try lifting the pony's tummy up underneath them each stride.

   The analogies of 'polishing' and 'being glued' might seem contradictory, but the advice depends on circumstances. A good teacher can explain concepts in many different ways. A child who moves too much in the saddle can be told to 'glue' to the saddle, whereas one who sits rooted and therefore bounces, can be told to 'polish' the saddle in order to develop the light swing necessary. The aim for the end result is the same – a light, but deep and secure seat that moves with the pony in balance.

3 Once the rider is secure in their position in the canter, even at the point when they are still holding the saddle for the transition, they can be taught to apply the aids for canter.

4 Begin by working in sitting trot, showing the rider how to move the legs into

Holding the saddle when beginning to canter.

the correct position to apply the aids. The inside leg remains on the girth, the outside leg is moved back slightly behind the girth. Once the rider can achieve this, they are ready to apply the aids to canter, with the support of the instructor, who takes a supervisory role over the transition.

DEVELOPING THE CANTER

AIMS

Aims when developing canter:
To increase the depth and security in the position, and therefore the effectiveness of the aids.

To increase the rider's ability to 'feel' the canter. Initially the canter will feel fast to the rider. This is because they are used to the speed of the walk and trot. Gradually they will become used to the feel of the canter. They will begin to feel when the quality of the canter is weakening, and understand that the pony requires a little more leg at this moment to maintain energy, in the same way that they learnt this about the trot.

To gradually increase the complexity of the exercises, in order to develop the rider and/or pony.

EXERCISES

The following is a list of exercises to develop the canter.

1 A few steps of canter.

2 Cantering from the corner along the following long side. Try to make the downward transition before the next corner, as cantering around the corner to begin with can unbalance the rider.

3 Cantering large. Teach the rider to maintain balance with the pony around the corners. Often the pony will become long and flat along the long sides of the

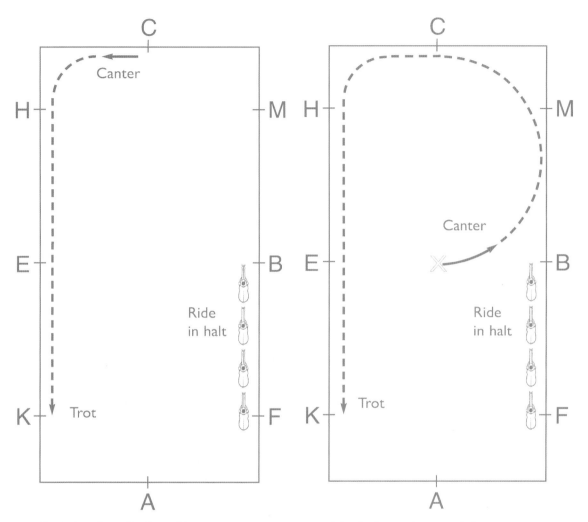

Cantering down the long side.   Introducing canter on a circle.

school, so the rider must be taught to maintain a steady contact on the reins, and keep the pony's energy with their legs, in order to help maintain balance and rhythm.

4 Trotting a 20m circle, make a canter transition just after X. Complete the circle and continue large in canter, This is a good exercise for introducing circles into the rider's canter work. By making the canter transition just after X, the pony should then follow the boards of the school to complete the circle and then go large. This gives the child the feel of cantering around part of the circle, before they take on the complete responsibility for steering around a circle.

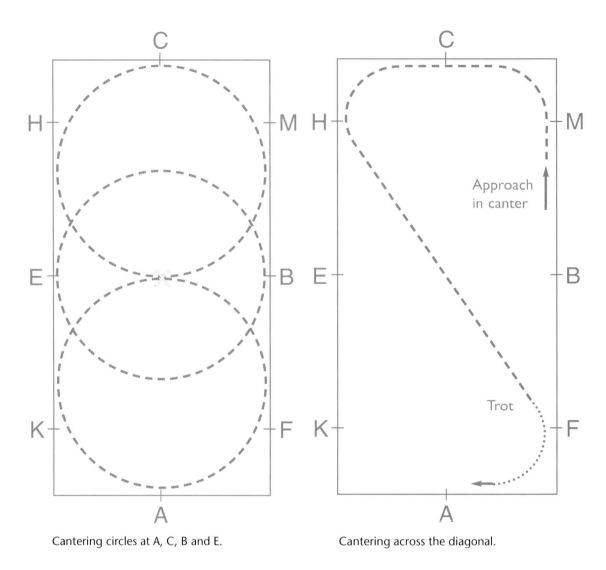

Cantering circles at A, C, B and E.   Cantering across the diagonal.

5   Canter 20m circles at A, B, C and E. Once the previous exercise has given
    the rider the feel for circles, then progress to cantering circles at A, B, C and
    E. The circles at A and C are generally easier as the pony has the boards of the
    school to support him for half the circle, so begin with these, then the circles
    at E and B.

6   Canter across the long diagonal, with a trot transition on reaching the track.
    Before this exercise, it is a good idea to practise cantering on an inner track.
    In this way pupils learn not to be dependent on and supported by the boards
    of the school.
        The areas to focus on with this exercise is to ride a balanced turn that takes

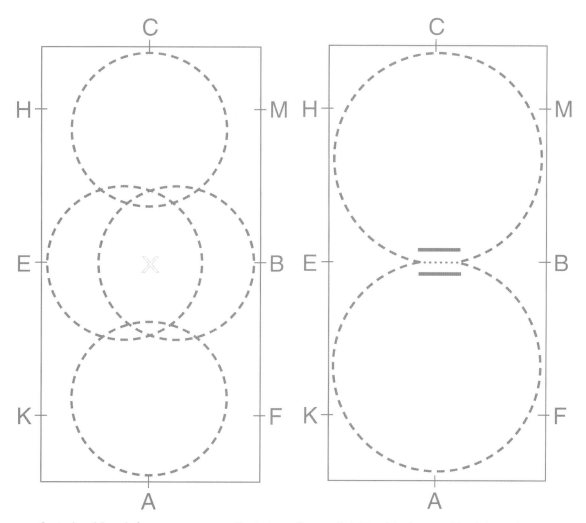

Cantering 15m circles.   Cantering a figure of eight, with change of lead through trot.

the pony on to the correct line, to prepare sufficiently for the downward transition, and to rebalance the trot quickly if necessary before riding through the corner.

7   Cantering 15m circles. At this point the rider should be able to ride good upward and downward transitions and control the pony both going large and on 20m circles. They should have a balanced and secure position, and be able to maintain a good rhythm in the canter, and so ride from leg to hand. Riding smaller circles will further increase their ability to ride the canter accurately. It will further develop the feel for the need of greater leg to hand connection to keep the pony balanced around a smaller circle.

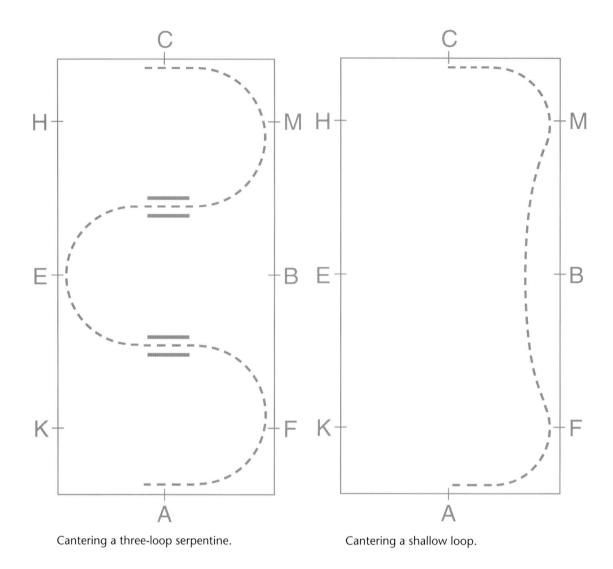

Cantering a three-loop serpentine.   Cantering a shallow loop.

8   Cantering a figure of eight with a change of lead leg through trot, over X. For this exercise, focus the rider on making a balanced downward transition, smooth change of bend, and a responsive upward transition. Initially, the exercise will require several steps of trot to achieve this, but as the rider becomes more accomplished, the number of trot steps will decrease until 3-4 are sufficient. Use poles over X to help guide the rider.

9   Cantering a three-loop serpentine, with changes of lead through trot, over the centre line. This exercise is similar to the figure of eight, but requires a smaller half circle at the end of each loop when ridden in a 20x40m arena. It therefore

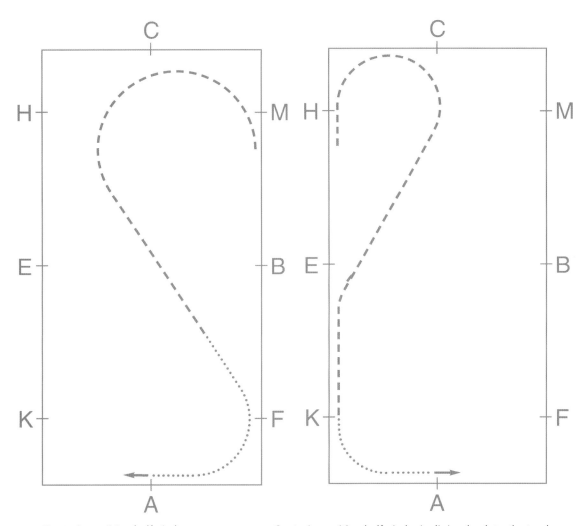

Cantering a 15m half-circle.

Cantering a 10m half-circle, inclining back to the track.

requires a shorter canter and teaches greater leg to hand connection. The exercise also contains two changes of leading leg, one swiftly following the other, so a good degree of organisation and forward thought are required. Again, use poles to guide the rider.

10 Cantering a 1m shallow loop, gradually building up to a 5m shallow loop. This exercise introduces counter-canter. Explain the need to maintain the correct bend for the canter throughout the exercise. By starting with a very shallow loop, the rider develops a feel for maintaining the bend and moving the pony back to the track without pulling on the reins and changing the bend. The depth of loop can be gradually increased.

11 Cantering a 15m half-circle, inclining back to the track with a transition to trot between X and the track. This exercise is a development from cantering across the diagonal and includes the greater challenge of the 15m half-circle, but the same principles apply as within that exercise – the turn on to the correct line, maintaining the correct bend in the canter, preparation for the transition and rebalancing before the corner.

12 Cantering a 10m half-circle, inclining back to the track before the end of the long side. Make a transition to trot at the end of the long side. An increase in level of difficulty, this exercise develops from the previous one. The counter-canter at the end of the diagonal line is easier to introduce in a 20x60m arena if you have access to one, as the counter-canter can be established for longer, giving greater preparation time for the downward transition.

For novice pupils, exercises 1-4 are likely to be used regularly for the canter work for the first few weeks or months, depending on how frequently they ride. Ensure that equal time is spent on both reins to develop a balanced rider, as well as symmetry in the pony. It is very easy to become 'stuck' and to try to perfect the same exercises in the canter before moving on, and although we do not wish to over-challenge the riders and cause loss of confidence, often moving on to the next level of difficulty teaches riders a new aspect of cantering that they can then take back to the easier exercises. (This is true of exercises in the trot also.)

A good source of inspiration for new canter exercises is to look at the way in which they develop in dressage tests.

7

Introducing dressage

'Flatwork' is a term we commonly use within riding schools to mean that we are riding on the flat, and are therefore not jumping or lungeing. 'Dressage' is derived from French and can be defined as training or preparation, usually associated with the horse and a capable rider who is able to influence the horse in a beneficial manner. We would not, therefore, say that a beginner rider was taking dressage lessons. However, once the rider is able to influence the pony in a positive way, it is helpful use the term 'dressage' for their lessons, as it removes some of the mystique associated with the term.

Explaining the scales of training

The simplest way to develop an understanding of the pony's way of going is to introduce the rider to the scales of training. *The scales of training are the foundation of the instructor's armoury to teach dressage positively and with cohesive structure.*

Rhythm

Rhythm and balance go hand in hand. You cannot have one without the other. Rhythm is a regular beat. In the case of riding, this is a regularity of the stride – the beat and balance of every stride.

School figures are excellent for teaching rhythm, especially serpentines, which highlight when the rhythm is lost. Children learn through 'doing', therefore, let them try the exercises and keep explanations simple, using basic language. An understanding of riding theory develops through practice. A rider might get a basic grasp of a concept when it is first explained, and the concept gains in depth and value when it is seen, but these things happen especially when it is felt. So, when a pupil rides a serpentine, ask them to feel if the pony speeds up or slows down, and whether there is a pattern to when the rhythm is lost. If they can feel and identify these areas, then you are helping them to develop the ability to

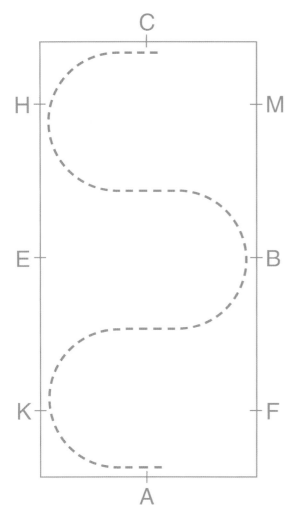

School figures such as serpentines are excellent for teaching pupils about rhythm.

analyse whilst riding. Then you teach the rider how to make improvements.

School figures such as serpentines are excellent for teaching pupils about rhythm.

Transitions can also highlight times when the rhythm is maintained or lost. If the pony moves effortlessly from one gait to the next, maintaining rhythm throughout, the transition has been balanced. If he takes a few strides to regain balance, the rider knows that the transition was unbalanced, and can then aim to improve the transition with the instructor's help. This work helps to give the rider a strong foundation of understanding what they are aiming for; to develop a feel for the pony's correct way of going.

RELAXATION AND LOOSENESS

Relaxation is the foundation for training. Mental relaxation puts pony and rider into the right frame of mind to be receptive to furthering their training. Also, mental relaxation leads to physical relaxation in both the pony and rider. In the pony, it helps the muscles to be free and supple and allows engagement of the hind legs to work 'through' the back, connecting or 'uniting' the rear and front ends. The rider should be encouraged to feel and allow this free movement.

The instructor must teach the rider to think about the temperament of the pony. If a child has their own highly strung pony, it is unrealistic to think that the rider can put him into a state of mental relaxation without first using up some excess energy. In all cases, the role of the instructor is to teach the rider to understand how to step into the pony's mind in order to work with him. Also, help riders to develop an understanding of why you have selected certain exercises, so that they, too, develop a repertoire to try with different ponies, or in different circumstances. For example, a pony who is usually relaxed may start off excitable in the wind, and a normal warm-up plan may have to be adapted to accommodate this. An explanation about why this is done will further develop the child's understanding.

CONTACT

Contact is the feeling along the reins. It is the result of the balance of the rest of the pony's body. An influential factor in this is the rider's position. The contact should feel consistent and light. If the pony feels too light or heavy in the reins, there is an imbalance in the rest of his body that needs to be addressed. A helpful method of explaining contact is to show the rider what they should feel down the reins by having them at one end of some reins and you at the other, whilst in halt.

A pony starting to stretch in the walk.

Useful explanations to help the rider understand contact are:

Following the early warm-up in walk, cantering in a light seat can assist both looseness and impulsion.

- 'Contact' is the feel through the reins between the rider and pony.
- The contact develops from the pony pushing his energy, produced in the hindquarters, forwards, over his back to the contact provided by the rider.
- The contact should be consistent unless/until the rider makes a conscious decision to change it briefly to produce a desired effect.
- The pony should seek the contact, feeling that he is moving forward, into it.
- The pony should trust the rider's hands enough that he wants to seek the contact.
- The contact, as well as other aids, can be used to help the pony to be balanced.
- If the contact feels 'wrong' at the end of the reins, the correction must come

69

from finding the problem elsewhere in the pony. The contact is a product of the pony's way of going.

■ The pony should never be forced to work into a manufactured outline. With correct training, the pony will naturally carry himself in a correct outline.

IMPULSION

Impulsion is contained energy; a desire to move forwards. It is particularly reflected in the pony's moment of suspension, and therefore the term is only used in connection with trot and canter, as the walk has no moment of suspension.

Propulsive energy is produced by the pony's hindquarters. The rider helps the pony to use this energy to produce springy and elastic steps, connecting the pony's rear and front ends through a springy back. When the pony has impulsion, he looks 'elastic' and the moment of suspension in trot and canter is pronounced – longer in time and heightened, with the pony's joints flexing more acutely. If the rider allows the pony to become too fast, the pony looks 'flat', and there is less time for the moment of suspension.

The converse of a pony moving with impulsion is one who is inactive and unresponsive to the rider's leg aids ('behind the leg'); lacking impulsion he will drag his feet, and there will be little in the way of suspension.

Good exercises to help the rider develop a feel for impulsion are well-ridden transitions and shortening and lengthening the stride.

STRAIGHTNESS

There are two terms used when discussing straightness – 'true' and 'relative' straightness. A pony is truly straight on a straight line when his hind legs follow the forelegs. Relative straightness refers to a pony who is 'straight' on a circle, that is,

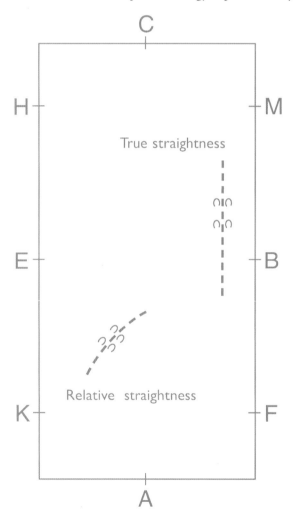

True and relative straightness.

the curve is even along the whole body and the hind legs are following the line of the forelegs, both hind and fore being on the same size circle.

Horses and ponies, like people, favour their right or left side. As riders, we try to develop our mount evenly on both sides, helping him to be equally supple in both directions. Apart from other benefits, this means that all the energy generated in his hindquarters can be used to push his body straight forwards. A straight pony will thus use himself better, with even pressure over his limbs and back. (As a human analogy, imagine the difference in riding a bicycle with a straight frame, as compared to one with a bent frame.) One important attribute of straightness is that a pony must be straight in order to be able to collect himself.

The best method of teaching riders about straightness is in a school with mirrors. Ask the rider to walk away from the mirrors, on an inner track and to try to feel whether the pony is straight or crooked, and where the crookedness is. Then ride the same exercise towards the mirror so that they can see what they have hopefully felt. Repeat the exercise in trot and canter, but note that horses and ponies have a natural tendency to canter with their quarters in slightly. As they become stronger, they are able to become straighter.

Classical exercises to aid straightening are shoulder-in and counter-canter. The rider therefore needs to be fairly capable to make an improvement in their pony's straightness.

COLLECTION

The rider and pony must be at a significant level in their training in order to start to work towards collection.

A pony naturally carries more of his weight on the forehand. By adding the weight of the rider closer to the front, we put more weight on the forelegs. Through correct training, muscles in the pony's hindquarters, and also in his back become stronger, which allows him to carry more weight on the hind legs and thus 'lighten' the forehand. This is the start of collection. Through gradual, progressive training, the pony is taught to carry more weight behind. This gives the feeling and visual impression that the pony is working 'uphill'. In collection, the strides become shorter in terms of ground covered, but the steps remain active and become higher through greater flexion of the joints.

When teaching dressage at the lower levels, focus the rider on the first three elements of the scales of training. Only when these are established can the pony and rider move further on.

A crooked pony.

A pony working nicely from leg into hand.

RIDING DRESSAGE TESTS

When teaching any rider regularly, it is important to set goals. One of these is entering a competition, no matter how large or small it may be. This allows riders to put their skills to the test, and gives the lessons that follow a new goal, keeping the teaching fresh. If you do not have access to 'official' competitions, maybe you know a judge who would be willing to come to the yard where you are teaching, to judge, or maybe there is another instructor at the yard who could judge for you, and you could return the favour. If not, you can always video a test and download it online to enter a UK-wide online competition. These are becoming increasingly popular for people without their own transport. (Search for dressage tests online for more information.)

Practising dressage in a relaxed lesson atmosphere is a world away from riding a test in competition. The psychological effect of competing is covered in Chapter 10. This chapter covers physically riding the test and how to teach riders to do so to the best of their abilities.

TIPS ON TRAINING FOR DRESSAGE TESTS

- Allow sufficient preparation time – the rider must go in well prepared. They may want the test read ('commanded') on the day in case of nerves, but they should know it well enough so that, during practise, they do not require it to be read. This is good training for all riders.
- Break the test down into bite-size chunks. Practise elements, then ride them with the movement before and after to make the test flow. In this way, riders practise entering and exiting their movements, creating links throughout the test.
- Teach the rider that the pony's way of going and their own position are the main priorities at all times.
- Teach the rider how to maximise marks in strong areas and minimise the loss in weak areas.
- Children are very 'black and white', and often if one part of the test goes wrong, they dwell on it and lose confidence. Teach them to focus on the next movement and ride it positively.
- Practise riding in their competition clothes.
- Have them ride practise tests with you as judge. Be as objective and positive as possible with your comments.
- Teach them to always finish the test with a smile to the judge!

8

INTRODUCING JUMPING

**See the appendix at the end of the book
for a table of jump distances.**

There is a tendency for riders to want to disassociate dressage and showjumping, and yet the two are integrally linked, with skills learnt on the flat taken into jumping. Equally, correct jumping can help to develop athleticism and strength and improve the pony's gaits. In some countries in Europe, child riders must have attained a certain level in dressage before they are allowed to compete in showjumping. This is how they emphasise the importance of dressage when jumping.

Most children are really quite keen to try jumping. Again, if the rider has been taught at a riding school, they are likely to have been introduced to jumping position and pole-work almost immediately, and therefore are on the developmental ladder that creates the foundation of their jumping. A novice rider can have many lessons working on position and course riding without going over anything but poles. This allows the rider to concentrate on these aspects of jumping without becoming distracted by the fences.

ASSESSING THE PONY'S CANTER

Within a riding school, the ponies should be continually schooled to improve all aspects of their work, including the canter. A rider is limited by what they can improve within an hour's lesson, and the majority of riding school clients are novice riders and are not in the position to make those improvements anyway. Generally, this is not the case for the child who rides their own pony, as even a more novice rider can learn to help their pony over time.

The canter is the most crucial gait for the showjumping pony. Although there are exceptions, usually a pony who canters well, can jump. It is the rider's (and therefore the instructor's) job to help the pony to produce the best canter possible, thus giving him the capability to jump to the best of his ability. There are many exercises to improve the pony's canter. The following points cover general aspects of the canter that you may come across when teaching.

THE 'WHIZZY' PONY

These ponies are usually seen wearing every gadget imaginable, with their head still in the air! Confident children like forward-thinking ponies, and unless they have been schooled by an adult, these ponies are often 'buzzed up' by the children riding them. If you are small enough, try riding the pony to see where the problem lies. Try adjusting feed, changing tack (the pony might actually go better in a softer bit), change the schooling and work around jumps on the flat sometimes, and include quiet hacking. Try walking when the pony becomes too excited, to allow the adrenalin to dissipate. In this way, such ponies do not become used to jumping in an excited state. Most importantly, try to keep the rider calm, and do not let them become too excited about jumping, as this will transfer to the pony.

THE BACKWARD-THINKING PONY

Again, look at tack, feed, rider confidence and schooling routine. Try to add variety to the work if they have become stale from jumping too frequently. Suggest that the pony is taken somewhere to have a good canter, preferably with a forward-thinking pony they can follow. Since competitive jumping takes place all year round, the pony might actually benefit from a little time off.

DISUNITED CANTER

This may be the result of a weak canter, or a physical problem. Once the physical side has been eliminated by the vet, then work to improve the canter. (Sometimes when the rider's hand is too strong and the canter is 'shut down' the pony will become disunited.) Ensure that the canter is ridden forwards. Have the rider canter in jumping position to lighten the weight effect on the pony's back, and take the pony cantering in fields and over undulating terrain as this will develop strength and balance.

STEPS TOWARDS JUMPING
JUMPING POSITION

The position should form the rider's security and balance when jumping. Adopted correctly, it has the ability to help the pony during a jump but, adopted incorrectly, it can both hinder the pony and reduce the rider's security. To reach an approximate correct length of stirrup leathers for jumping, the rider should have right angles at their knees when their feet are in the stirrups with the heels down. Often, this is roughly two holes shorter than their dressage length.

ELEMENTS OF JUMPING POSITION
- Stirrups on the balls of the feet with the heels down, without allowing the lower legs forward.
- The lower legs wrapped around the pony's sides. This is where the security in the position comes from.
- As the rider folds forward, keeping the back straight, the seat is pushed towards the back of the saddle.
- The rider lifts up, hovering above the saddle.
- As well as holding the reins, the rider holds a section of mane close to the saddle. The mane is held initially to assist with balance, to prevent the rider from balancing on the reins or catching the pony in the mouth. As the rider develops balance in the jumping position, they will need the mane less. However, it is important to stress that many riders of international standard hold the mane in times of crisis, and it is acceptable at any level when necessary.

Riders should find their own point of balance, so that in halt, if they let go of the mane, they remain balanced. From the outset, make sure that the rider does not grip with their knees. Gripping with the knees leads to the rider losing security with the lower leg, which then moves backwards, tipping the rider's upper body forwards.

Introducing jumping position at an early stage builds a foundation for jumping later on.

EXERCISES IN JUMPING POSITION
The aim is to try to make the rider as proficient in jumping position as they are in their dressage position.

For lead-rein and first ridden
- Jumping position first in walk, then introducing short periods of trot along the long side.
- Gradually build up the amount of work in jumping position.
- Teach riders how to use the legs to maintain the walk or trot.

■ Start to introduce a basic 20m circle in jumping position and show the rider how to steer with one hand, whilst holding the mane with the other. Explain how they can swap hands when necessary. Riding school movements in jumping position gives riders the opportunity to practise finding their balance and independence within their position before introducing jumps.

For children at a higher standard
In jumping position:

■ Teach them how to use their legs to maintain energy and rhythm in the gait.
■ Start to include a variety of school figures in trot.
■ Start to include transitions.
■ Introduce canter, then school figures and changes of rein in the canter with changes of leading leg through trot.

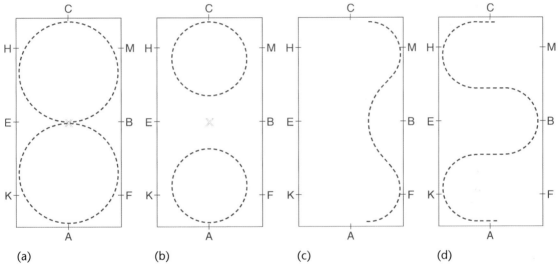

School figures to be ridden in trot in jumping position: (a) 20m circles, (b) 15m circles; (c) shallow loop; (d) three-loop serpentine.

POLE-WORK

Pole-work exercises are valuable for teaching children about jumping, without actually jumping. The rider needs to develop the skills to think and jump at the same time, and the poles are good stepping stones before fences. A great deal of time can be spent teaching riders about maintaining rhythm and balance, and riding the correct line before fences are introduced.

It is very easy to overwhelm children with information, in jumping more so than dressage, as there is an enormous amount to think about in a short space of time. However, all elements can slot neatly within two headings:

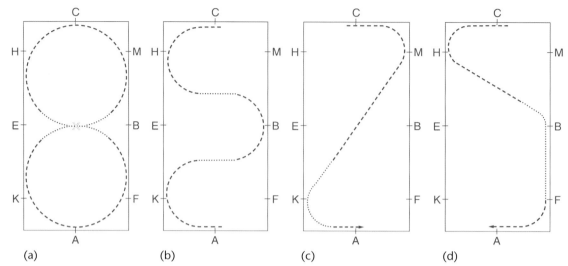

School figures to be ridden in canter (with lead changes through trot) in jumping position: (a) figure of eight; (b) three-loop serpentine; (c) change rein across the long diagonal; (d) change rein across a short diagonal.

Rhythm
- Consistent speed.
- Maintaining the pony's balance.
- Response to the aids.

Lines
- Looking ahead to see the fence/poles, where to turn, and the line of departure.
- Turning on to the line that takes the pony at right angles to the fence/poles (unless it is a jump-off turn).
- Ride a straight line to the centre of the fence and, on departure from the fence. Use the correct amount of space in the arena in order to rebalance the pony and re-establish the rhythm if necessary in order to ride a good approach to the next fence.

Experienced instructors who teach children, keep things simple and use language that they understand. Give clear, short instructions that identify the root of the problem, and therefore also solve peripheral problems arising from this.

POLE EXERCISES
These involve gradual increases in difficulty.

1 **Single and treble poles on an inner track at E/B**. You should help the riders to know when to turn by positioning a cone that they must ride around. Create a runway towards and away from the poles using ground-poles, with a cone to turn around as they reach the other side. Gradually lessen the help

given to the rider – remove guide poles and eventually cones. The key points to teach with this exercise are rhythm and lines:

- Look ahead.
- Control the pony by applying the aids correctly.
- Keep the pony straight on the approach, over, and away from the pole(s).
- Maintain the same rhythm. Problem areas in this respect include the initial turn, over the pole and the second turn.

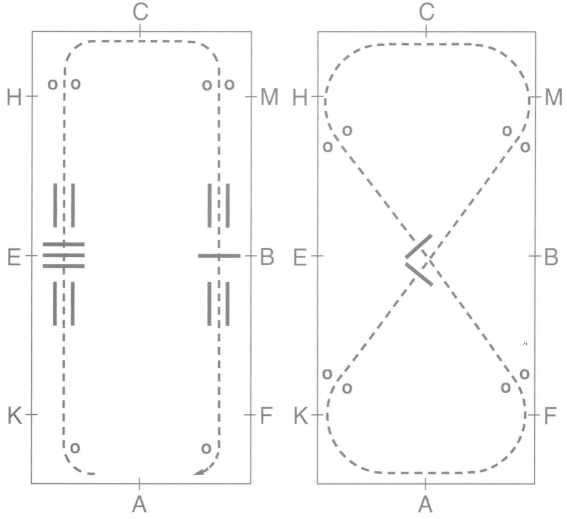

Single and treble trotting-poles.   Poles on a figure of eight.

2 **Poles on a figure of eight**. This is the first exercise on the way to riding around a course. Use cones to help the child to know when to turn. This exercise

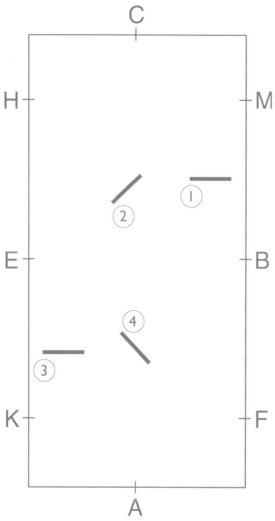

Using poles to lay out a short course.

requires good visualisation skills as the rider is turning on to lines that do not run parallel to the sides of the school.

A key point is that pupils learn to ride a good line through the centre of the poles.

3 Poles to make a short course. This is a natural extension from the previous exercise. It can be ridden in trot for novice riders, taking jumping position over the poles; children with rather more experience can ride the whole course in jumping position out of trot. The most established riders can ride the exercise in canter, organising their change of leading leg at the appropriate time, and they could ride the whole course in jumping position.

Teach the riders when to make the most balanced changes of leading leg as they ride around the course (in the corner after the second pole in the diagram). Stress that the rider must set up the canter before the approach for the next pole.

INTRODUCING SMALL FENCES

The fences can remain very small (30cm cross-poles) for as long a period as necessary. The aim when you introduce jumping is that it naturally flows on from the work that you have already done with poles. By the time a rider jumps they should be able to:

■ Ride good lines around a course of poles without needing cones or ground-poles to guide them.
■ Identify when, and possibly why, they lose rhythm.

SOME JUMPING EXERCISES
The following are two introductory jumping exercises.

1 Trotting-poles into a fence. In order to introduce the rider to jumping safely, the instructor must make the jump simple for the pony. Using trotting-poles into a fence will do this.

- Teach the child to ignore the fence and treat it as an exercise that they have already ridden with poles. Focus the child on the rhythm and line.

- As the rider begins to jump, they must learn to hold themselves off the pony's back. Explain how the joints – ankle, knee and hip – soften to absorb the movement. Explain the purpose of jumping position – to keep the weight of the rider off the pony's back and to stay in balance with him in order for the pony to make the best possible jumping effort.

2 **Developing poles into fences**. Use pole exercises 2 and 3 above, substituting ground-poles for small cross-poles. Most ponies will trot happily over small fences, and more experienced riders can work in canter over small cross-poles.

GRIDWORK

Grids can be constructed to offer a highly valuable series of exercises that can introduce riders to:

- Riding over more than one fence in quick succession.
- Different types of fences and fillers.
- Maintaining the rhythm between fences.
- Maintaining their position and balance between fences.
- 'Feel' for a stride.
- 'Feel' for riding related distances.

EXERCISES WITH GRIDS

The following basic grid exercises are shown in the accompanying diagrams:

- one stride
- one stride to one stride
- one stride to two strides
- one stride to three strides

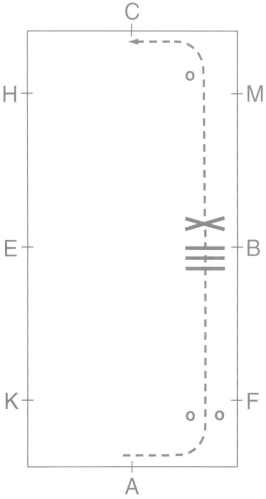

Trotting-poles into a fence.

Trotting over three poles.

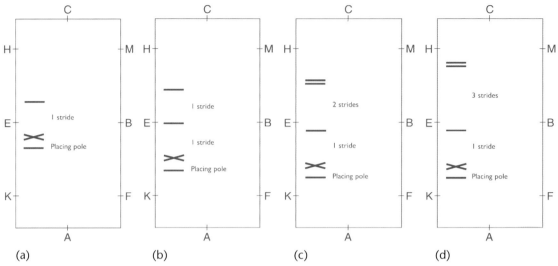

(a) (b) (c) (d)

Some basic grids: (a) one stride between two elements; (b) one stride to one stride; (c) one stride to two strides; (d) one stride to three strides.

POINTERS FOR TEACHING GRIDWORK

The following is good practice when building grids:

- Approaching in trot is generally safer than canter, as the pony is more likely to reach a good point of take-off in trot, and is therefore more likely to be well balanced in the grid.

- Encourage the pony and rider into the centre of the grid by using a cross-pole as the first element.

- When warming up over fences, the pony should have jumped a cross-pole first, then a vertical, then a spread. Once this has been done, it is appropriate to use a mixture of verticals and spreads in the grid.

- Alternate the rein of approach each lesson.

Gridwork. The rider has raised her hand a little, but is not interfering with the pony's mouth.

JUMPING A COURSE

Practising the various elements of jumping can be tested by riding a course. Again, this is a natural progression from the courses of poles and little jumps mentioned earlier. A basic course can be built simply with four jumps, or a longer course can be planned using the same four jumps, or a more complex course of eight to ten jumping efforts can be laid out using just six fences.

Riding around eight fences requires greater mental concentration than around four fences. This often becomes a hurdle for children to overcome – and just remembering the course may be an issue initially. Only practice can improve this.

Remember each child's learning style. A child who has auditory learning skills would be a better candidate to go first in a group, leaving the visual ones to watch someone else riding it first.

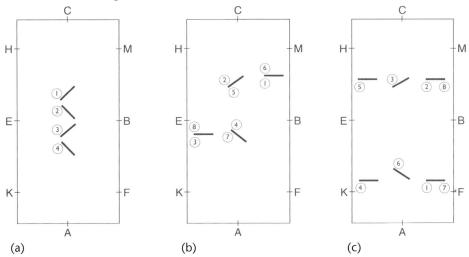

It only takes a few obstacles to produce an interesting and challenging course: (a) a four-fence course, with changes of rein; (b) an eight-fence course using just four obstacles; (c) an eight-fence course using six obstacles.

With practice and experience, pupils will hopefully progress to the level of course shown here.

9

INTRODUCING CROSS-COUNTRY

There are some riding schools that do not have the facilities for riding outside. There are many others, however, that have a cross-country course, or at least a field where some fences can be erected so instructors, whether employed by these centres or freelance, will often teach outside. This is particularly applicable to instructors who teach for the Pony Club. It is 'real life', after all, and often we are rather detached from such reality within the cocoon of an arena.

Teaching outside can be an anxious time for instructors initially. There are valid reasons for this, and risk assessments must be made to reduce these risks to a minimum. However, if you teach children and their mounts in a field regularly, it becomes normal for all involved, losing the element of excitement for pony and child.

The key point to understand is that riding outside is a big milestone for pupils. Children find it very enjoyable, but would not be aware at first that their ponies may behave differently in a field from the way they behave in the school. The instructor initially has to reduce the complexity of exercises ridden when outside in order to maintain control and reduce risk and it is the instructor's responsibility to teach children that the ponies may behave differently, and introduce the new challenges of riding outside.

MOTIVES AND RISK ASSESSMENT

An initial point to be clear about is the key reason why you are taking the riders outside. For example, is it to add a little variety to the lessons, to make general progress with a class, or are you teaching a competitive child on their own pony? Your goals and approach to planning the lessons will be different depending upon the circumstances.

The risks of riding outside can be minimised by:
- Taking the ponies into the field regularly. This reduces the excitement factor for the ponies and children at being outside: it becomes normal.

- Schooling the ponies outside regularly with staff or more experienced riders.
- Ensuring that the children have ridden their ponies regularly in an arena beforehand, and are confident on them.
- For riders within a riding school, setting guidelines for the level required before the rider can ride outside. A suggested minimum would be walk, trot, canter and 76cm (2ft 6in) jump. This shows a good level of experience. (However, if there are competent leaders, it can add a little variety to take lead-rein riders into the field.)
- Riding in the field on the flat regularly before contemplating jumping outside. The riders must have as much control and confidence in the field as in the school, before jumping.
- Assessing conditions; the weather should be calm and the ground conditions suitable – not slippery or hard.
- Keeping numbers in a group to a practical minimum.
- Using tack that gives appropriate control to the rider.
- Insisting that riders wear a hat without a peak, and a fitted body protector.
- Unless you are teaching a child on a very independent pony, or are within sight of other horses, try not to go into the field in a private lesson, as the pony may become unsettled on his own. Equally, try not to teach near external influences which may excite the pony, such as next to a field of turned out ponies.

RIDING IN A FIELD

Learning to ride in the open has to be taught. It is a skill, just like all other aspects of riding. Try to use a small, flat field initially if possible.

- Teach the riders that the size of the field can influence the ponies to go faster, which means that they must keep their ponies under control.
- In due course, discuss the effect of gradient on the gaits. The ponies may become quicker downhill, and may put more or less effort into travelling uphill, depending on their breeding.
- Discuss the point that riding towards or away from home can have an effect on the pony's speed, and this simulates the circumstances that they might find if they went competing. Moving towards or away from the warm-up arena or lorry park can have the same effect.
- Keep exercises simple; walk and trot only until you are certain that the riders have complete control and are confident.
- Structure the lessons so that pupils build on what they have done before, developing the trot work before introducing the canter.

- When introducing the canter, ensure it is away from home, towards other ponies and that the other riders are in walk.
- The canter work can be gradually increased.
- Once the riders are competent enough, you can start to work them in open order in the field, beginning in walk and trot, developing the work to include canter. This simulates warming up for outdoor showjumping or cross-country competition.
- At this point the riders are ready to be introduced to 'gears' in the canter and then to jumping outside.

Learning to ride happily and with confidence in the open is the foundation for riding cross-country.

Introducing 'gears'

Jumping one or two straightforward fences in a field to add variety to school lessons is different from preparing a rider for a cross-country course. For a rider to have the ability to ride safely around a cross-country course, they must be able to change the pony's canter. It is quite common to find riders who just school in a 20x40m arena, and hack on the roads. Many riders (including pony owners) are not used to working in more than a showjumping canter, because they simply do not have the facilities.

At first, riding at higher speeds can be unnerving for riders, and their ponies may feel unbalanced. The canter work needs to be developed so that balance is achieved at cross-country speeds.

As the canter moves up through the gears, it increases in energy and length of stride. For both pony and rider, learning to remain in balance and mutual harmony takes time to achieve, especially if the pair are only used to working on a level surface. Interestingly, this process and the work involved will usually help the showjumping and dressage canter. The pony becomes stronger and more balanced in general.

When introducing the concept of varying the canter, keep things simple at first – divide the canter into three gears:

1 **Showjumping canter** – relatively short and bouncy, approximately 350mpm.
2 **Hacking canter** – covers the ground with an easy stride, approximately 400mpm.
3 **'Galloping' canter** – longer stride, approximately 450mpm.

Going up and down hills is part and parcel of riding cross-country.

450mpm is Intro and Pre-Novice speed. Generally, at first, gears one and two will be the ones used for jumping, and gear three for in between the fences, where appropriate. As your rider becomes a more experienced competitor, the speed can be increased in a sensible and appropriate way.

There are two methods of teaching the rider about speeds – either they train beside an experienced pony and rider combination to gain a feel for the speed, or a training distance is marked out and the rider and instructor work with a stopwatch. The choice of method depends on facilities and other riders being available to assist with teaching speeds. Once the child has a feel for the speeds on fairly level terrain, then the same is taught on slight uphill and downhill slopes.

The rider's position is highly influential to the balance of the pony when riding cross-country. At all times, the lower leg provides the security within the position. The upper body can be utilised to aid in the control of the speed – bringing the upper body back will help to decrease the speed and or rebalance the pony on the approach to a fence. When riding downhill, the upper body is brought back to aid in the balance of the canter downhill. When riding uphill, the body will fold further forwards, maintaining balance of pony and rider at all times.

Part of the learning process of riding through gears in cross-country is practising thinking slowly and clearly at a faster speed. Often, children become swept up in the excitement of riding outside in canter and they must be able to think clearly and slowly before starting jumping. Ask them to analyse the canter or count strides whilst working through the gears to focus their thoughts. The next step is to introduce jumping in the gears in an arena.

Indoor 'cross-country'

Some cross-country fences can be simulated in the arena before riding them in the field. This will teach riders to approach fences on an angle, be accurate at narrow fences and to approach in a somewhat stronger canter than they may have ridden before. (However, when training in an arena, it is really only possible to go up to second gear in the canter, as the third requires more space and straighter lines than average sized arenas will allow.)

Exercises

For all of the following exercises, warm up as normal for jumping, checking jumping position and work over a cross-pole, vertical and spread first. The stirrup leathers may be taken shorter than showjumping length. With shorter stirrups, the rider is able to utilise their position to aid the balance of the partnership when jumping and between the fences. The movement of the rider is minimised with shorter stirrup leathers and therefore will impede the jump and canter of the pony less than longer leathers would. The pony can then be at his most efficient when jumping at faster speeds.

1 **Square oxer.** Build a square oxer at E or B and bring the rider in first and second gears over the fence. Teach them to keep their legs on into the fence and to ride away positively from the fence. This may save a valuable second at each fence in a competition, a total of 18–25 seconds around a full-length cross-country course.

Low but wide spread fences built with show jumps can develop confidence before tackling cross-country obstacles.

2 **Spreads in related distances**. The width (spread) of cross-country fences is often an initial concern to children. All cross-country fences have the potential to be rider frighteners, and this is a good exercise to introduce wider jumps before tackling real, solid cross-country fences.

For the above, keep the jumps well within the child and pony's comfort zone, building wider rather than higher to help the child and pony to become used to a wider fence without scaring them about the height. Start with single fences, approaching in first and then second gear, then include a second element in a related distance on a straight line, and a related distance on a dogleg. Teach the rider to maintain the rhythm and gear and commit to the fences.

3 **Narrow fences.** Now firmly established favourites with course-builders, narrow fences, or 'skinnies' as they are known, are easy fences to simulate in an arena. As they sometimes cause problems, there are advantages to practising indoors before trying them in a field.

As with any new fence, keep these small and simply built at first, well within both the child's and pony's comfort zone. First build the fence with guide rails to channel the pony into the narrow jump. The fence should be jumped out of first gear to gain the best accuracy. The guide rails can then be placed on the ground, before being removed completely.

OUTDOOR CROSS-COUNTRY

If you have access to a minimus course, you can introduce cross-country jumps straight away. If not, take a couple of showjumps outside for the children and ponies to get used to jumping in the field.

In the latter case, once they are used to jumping outside, you can introduce the cross-country fences. Select very simple, small, straightforward fences to begin with, preferably on the flat, or slightly uphill, with good groundlines. Little logs and rails tend to be the fences of choice at first. Make sure that the going on the approach and departure is good, and that the pony can see both. If you are working with a very confident pony, jump away from home; a

Three phases in learning to jump an arrowhead.

Out on the cross-country course.

less confident pony will benefit from jumping towards home. Explain to the child that they are going to begin in first gear when in canter. A very small log can be introduced in trot, before the canter.

Once the combination is confident over a couple of individual little fences, link two or three together. The rider must focus on maintaining the rhythm in the canter, and on the lines of approach. If it is safe to do so, try to link fences both towards and away from home so that the child can feel any difference that this produces in the canter, then help them to work towards maintaining the same speed.

The key to training pony and rider in all aspects of riding is to gradually introduce each step methodically and not to overface either pony or rider. Always finish whilst confidence is high. If you begin to think, 'Shall I just try this as well?' – don't! There will always be another day.

When introducing a green pony to cross-country fences, it is of benefit to have an experienced pony to assist as a lead. An experienced, confident rider rather than an novice rider should be on board when training the green pony.

As lessons progress, always re-cap, consolidate and then build on what you have already done. This is not just for the pony; it also makes the child more confident. It is better that they finish the lesson wanting more than creating anxiety for the next time.

DIFFERENT FENCES AND ASSESSING POSSIBLE REACTIONS

Whether teaching ponies, riders, or both, it is necessary for the instructor to have a good idea of the possible reactions different obstacles may invoke.

Log – a straightforward fence, which usually causes no problem.

Rails – a straightforward fence, which usually causes no problem.

Bullfinch – the pony jumps very high to clear the strands of birch, rather than jumping through them.

Steeplechase (or simulated hurdle)– an inviting fence, which usually would not cause problems.

Hedge – can look wide to the rider.

Drop – the rider can over-compensate and shorten the canter too much, leaving no energy to jump the fence. When first introduced, a positive trot approach can be more successful than canter. Riders can be taught to lean back over a drop whilst slipping the reins so as not to impede the pony. The rider must learn to stay off the pony's back even though they are leaning back slightly. This takes practice.

Stile – usually jumps well once practised.

Bank – usually jumps well once practised. Practise inidividual fences up and downhill before jumping a bank.Teach the rider to lean back (and slip the reins as necessary) during the jump off the bank, otherwise it may take them by surprise. As with the drop, initially approach in a positive trot as it can be ridden positively forward.

Steps – as with the bank. Jumping up at first is easier than down. Try to have pupils jump up one or two first, then link two or three together, and the same for downwards.

Corner – potentially encourages the pony to run out – practise in an arena first. When introducing corners, use ones that are not too wide, as a rider conscious of the prospect of a run-out may actually take a dangerous line over the widest part.

Narrow – potentially encourages the pony to run out – practise in an arena first. Because these fences are known to be difficult, the rider can actually try too hard and end up over-checking the canter, discouraging the pony. The fence must still be ridden positively. Always ride initially with guide poles, because if the pony starts to run out, it is hard to stop this habit.

Ditch – reactions vary to this obstacle. Some ponies will take it in their stride, whilst others will balk at the prospect of jumping it.

Coffin – daunting task to pony and rider when first encountered. It must be practised first by jumping elements individually if possible, then linking the second and third, then all three. A coffin should only be tackled once the pony and rider are confident with plain ditches.

Water – this is very much dependent upon whether the pony has a natural aversion to water. Introduction to water jumps is helped by a lead pony paddling through as an escort to get the pony used to walking, then trotting, then cantering through water. This may take a few sessions and it is always better to finish on a good note rather than pushing it too far. You never want the pony to say 'no'. Explain to riders about the 'drag effect' on the pony's movement through water.

Log

Rails

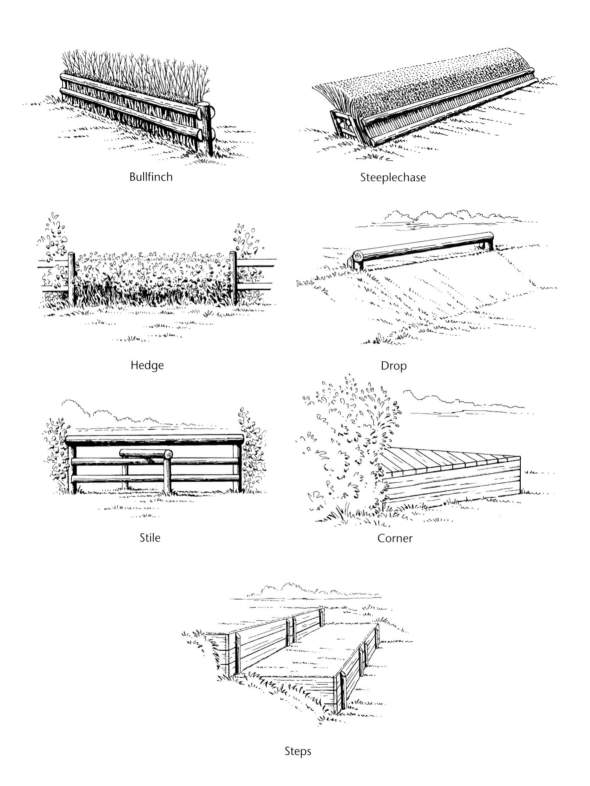

Bullfinch

Steeplechase

Hedge

Drop

Stile

Corner

Steps

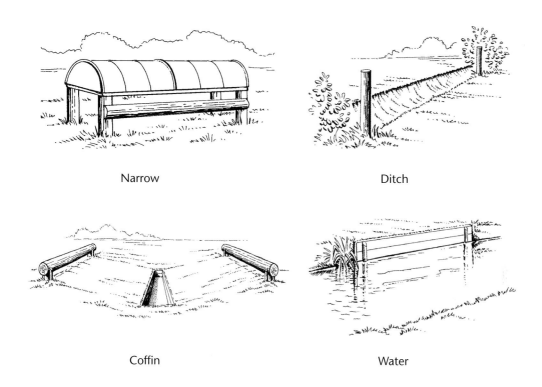

Narrow

Ditch

Coffin

Water

COURSE-WALKING AND EVALUATING APPROACHES

When assessing a cross-country course, whether it be a few fences in a lesson or a competition course, each obstacle needs to be assessed independently to decide on the line of approach and in which gait to approach. Since, for most obstacles, the gait will be canter, there is then the question of which canter 'gear'. A confident, experienced pony and rider will be able to approach a straightforward fence in a higher gear and then be able to reduce this as necessary for a downhill fence, a combination or a narrow obstacle. The overall aim is to maintain rhythm so far as possible, not only in respect of balance, but also to drain the least energy from both pony and rider. Stopping and starting saps energy. Anyone who runs will know that doing so at a certain speed is less tiring than accelerating and decelerating. Fighting the contact tires both child and pony. Ensure that the pony has the appropriate bit and tack to give the rider control. Teach the child to use the tack correctly and sympathetically.

When they first ride courses, advise pupils to ride at a speed that they and the pony are comfortable in, rather than aiming for a fast (or even a particular) time. As they become more experienced, they can adjust the speed accordingly. If they aim for a fast time initially, they will not be safe.

10

STARTING LITTLE COMPETITIONS

A clutch of rosettes ready to be given out.

Encouraging young riders to test their competence by way of competition is a natural step in a rider's career. It also follows the natural competitive instinct that most children possess and helps to develop new goals for lessons.

If you teach a child who does not want to or cannot compete, you can set other goals to aim for. Goal-setting is fundamental to good teaching. Short, medium and long term goals offer aims to be achieved or modified. They offer an opportunity to reflect on progress. 'Progression' can be assessed on many levels. It might be that initially the child was terrified at the thought of competing, but wanted to overcome that hurdle. Progress is then reflected in the achievement of taking part, rather than whether the rider returned with a red rosette.

If a child is interested in one of the three main disciplines, dressage, showjumping and eventing, an unaffiliated dressage competition would usually be the obvious choice as the first competition. You may be lucky in having access to a little unaffiliated competition locally, or you may teach at a centre that holds 'in-house' competitions. Alternatively, local shows usually include some fun showing classes, which give the rider and pony classes to enter with less pressure than learning a dressage test. This is a suitable way in which to introduce both child and pony to the atmosphere of competition, especially since such shows often include lead-rein classes.

Some riding schools 'hire' their ponies to clients to enable them to try in-house competitions, which is a lovely way for riders without their own ponies to gain a taste of competition, and is a good exercise in public relations for the riding school.

During these competitions, be they affiliated, unaffiliated, individual or team, every rider must learn that their ultimate responsibility is to their pony.

ORGANISING GRASS ROOTS COMPETITIONS

'NO PRESSURE' COMPETITIONS

Key elements for the 'no pressure' formula are:
- Every child goes home with a rosette.
- The competition is well organised.
- Rules are ideally accessible one month before the show.
- Children (and parents) are given help preparing.
- It is important to enlist the help of sympathetic judges for showing and dressage in early competitions.

The moment of success.

COMMITTEE RESPONSIBILITIES

Ask a small number of people with different strengths to join you to organise grass roots competitions to give the riders a solid foundation in competing. The following are the roles that will need to be allocated, and many can be doubled up.

Chairman – directs the organisation of the event: usually a knowledgeable person, who is capable of writing the rules if rules other than those in force for affiliated competitions are used.
Vice Chairman – support for the Chairman, and takes the Chairman's role in their absence.
Treasurer – manages finance.
Secretary – both on the day and dealing with advanced entries. The Secretary usually takes the minutes of the meetings also.
Rosettes – stocktaking, ordering and ensuring

A well-deserved achievement.

that they are ready on the day. (This role is often carried out by the secretary.)

Advertising – in-house or external. Many areas have sections in a local paper suitable for advertising local competitions externally. (This role is often carried out by the secretary.)

Course design /test/class selection – this position requires a knowledgeable person.

Course-building – on the day/day before, as appropriate. (This role requires a knowledgeable course-builder and willing helpers.

Stewards – at the competition, to make the event run smoothly.

Scorers – at the competition. Need a reasonable knowledge of the rules.

The planning meetings can be as formal or informal as you wish, but do take minutes and hand them out as a reminder of responsibilities volunteered for.

SUITABLE CLASSES
FUN SHOW

This could have classes such as the following:
- Prettiest face
- Most beautiful tail
- Pony the judge would most like to take home
- Handy pony
- Best turned out
- Best ridden

The last three classes could have score sheets, giving marks for each element that the judge is assessing. This makes the class less subjective, and gives feedback for the competitors to work on and improve – a good idea, even though it does entail a bit of extra work for the committee or judge.

By timetabling these competitions into school holidays, the competitors have the opportunity to spruce their pony up to make him sparkle!

Ready for the best turned out class.

DRESSAGE

British Dressage is the governing body for dressage in the UK. Affiliated tests and test sheets can be bought from them and used for unaffiliated competitions. The Pony Club also have their own dressage tests, including walk and trot tests. These can be purchased from the Club. For both societies, see Contacts at the end of the book.

Unaffiliated 'have-a-go' dressage competitions have become extremely popular. They have become an addition to many club level classes and often consist of walk and trot tests. This enables riders to enter a competition in smart, but not necessarily competition kit, often in tack that may not be 'legal' in affiliated classes. In an ideal world, all ponies would go well in a snaffle. However, for children who ride 'inherited' ponies in a strong bit, it gives them the opportunity to compete in a low-key, relaxed competition without feeling that they are going to lose control. This will hopefully give them the inspiration to work towards a snaffle for affiliated competition. 'Have-a-go' is a stepping stone, confidence-giving class, similar to clear round in showjumping.

Another inventive, 'no-pressure' idea, is to use bronze, silver and gold placings and rosettes rather than the traditional first to sixth. All riders in the same percentage bracket receive the same rosettes, for example 70+% gold, 60–69.9% silver, 50–59.9% bronze. Specials can be given to those who had a bad day with under 50%!

As the children develop their competition skills, they will move on from walk and trot tests, to unaffiliated Preliminary and Novice. At this stage, they may wish to affiliate, or at least try affiliation by competing on a ticket, which offers day membership to British Dressage for the exact reason that it gives riders the opportunity to try affiliated competition.

Before children reach this stage, in-house competitions could offer a class that forbids the calling ('commanding') of a test. Although tests can be read in most British Dressage competitions, they cannot in British Eventing, and learning to do without it is an extra stepping stone towards the greater pressure of affiliated competition.

SHOWJUMPING

The majority of young riders adore showjumping. Competitions can be designed (and courses built) relatively easily, incorporating clear round classes, where as much help as necessary can be given. (Ensure that the rules are clear about whether the rider achieves a clear round rosette if helped. These points regularly cause conflict purely because the rules are unclear. A 'special' rosette is often given if the rider was helped. An exception would be the lead-rein rider, who would achieve a clear round even though led.)

When considering classes, the height and technicality of the course is dependent upon the competitors. Be clear about whether the rider progresses directly into the jump-off if clear in the first round, known as 'Two Phase', or whether they leave the arena and return after all of the riders have completed the first round, known as A7.

Taking part in a lead-rein clear round.

British Showjumping (formerly the British Show Jumping Association) has introduced 'Training Classes' for juniors at competitions. Any rider in that particular class who rides clear in the first and second round, known as a 'double clear', takes joint first position. This encourages riders to ride with care in order to go clear, rather than fast, to beat the time. Other British Showjumping classes retain the jump-off against the clock. An in-house competition can reflect the same intentions, with a schedule that consists of classes similar to those below:

Clear Round – 50cm (1ft 8in) – see our rules for details: can be led.

Class 1 – 50cm (1ft 8in) Training Class – in accordance with British Showjumping rules.

Class 2 – 60cm (2ft) Training Class – in accordance with British Showjumping rules.

Class 3 – 70cm (2ft 4) Star Spotters – Two Phase – in accordance with British Showjumping rules.

Class 4 – 80cm (2ft 7in) Star Spotters – Two Phase – in accordance with British Showjumping rules.

HUNTER TRIALS

For many juniors, cross-country is one of the most thrilling activities in which to participate with their pony. To organise a hunter trial at grass roots level requires numerous, small, well-maintained cross-country fences, within a secure, well-maintained field. A lead-rein minimus course of about eight to ten jumps can also be included if the obstacles are small enough. The riders should have a good basic level of ability before being allowed to compete alone. A good class to include in the schedule is a pairs class. This allows a less experienced rider or pony to pair up with a more experienced combination, the latter giving a lead where necessary for their partner to gain confidence.

Almost certainly, even if the competition is in-house, your insurance cover will require adequate first aid in attendance, which increases the cost significantly. In fact, potentially everything related to organisation is carried out on a larger scale than for other competitions – jump judges on each fence, more scorers, catering, hiring flags and numbers to flag the courses, maps of the course(s), timing system. However, although it takes effort to bring the course up to

Waiting to start the cross-country course.

standard each time, it does mean that the course is maintained, allowing you to hire it out to Pony Clubs, Riding Clubs or individuals, as well as it being useful in lessons where appropriate.

A little like a 'Mini Badminton', each rider to complete could be given a rosette or token by which to remember the event.

TEAM COMPETITIONS

As children develop in confidence and ability, so they seek the next challenge. Being part of a team develops a different outlook on competition. No longer are they riding as individuals, but for the good of the team. This means that they have to ride to instructions from the captain or trainer. They may feel that they are sacrificing individual glory for the good of the team. When they lose, they learn to share the loss together, rather than blaming an individual. When they win, they win together, and sharing that experience is even better than individual achievement.

Being able to be a part of a team develops maturity, so it also encourages growth in the child.

DEALING WITH FRUSTRATION

The emphasis during early competitions must be enjoyment, fun and participation. By removing 'placings', as such, the pressure of competing is lessened. This is why bronze, silver and gold placings are so successful.

Inevitably, there will be times of frustration. Setbacks will occur throughout life, and from the perspective of the instructor this is an opportunity to teach pupils how to see them positively. This is very much part of the instructor's responsibility and is another skill to teach.

If riders are to learn and develop from disappointment, the first step is to accept the disappointment. This removes the element of frustration and allows the child to move forwards. This is the hard part and requires repeated training. Luckily (in some ways), we do not deal with disappointment regularly therefore, when it does happen, taking time to come to terms with it is important. Children first see things in black and white: something is good or bad. Then they try to blame – themselves, the pony, the judge. As the judge's decision is final, teach them to simply accept it. Acceptance may not happen at the time, but maybe it will a day later. Then you can help them to analyse the performance –

Frustration and disappointment are the 'down sides' of competing, but a good instructor will help pupils come to terms with these emotions, and learn from their experience.

Riders need to appreciate that their ponies may take time to adapt to a competition environment.

preparation, travel, warm-up, test or class, the way they treated everyone afterwards, their feelings throughout. Areas that they identify for improvement form the foundation for the next set of goals – short, medium and/or long term. Help the rider to see a method to achieving their aims. Turn what they perceived as a disappointment into a positive learning experience. Remind them that there are always more opportunities, and mini-setbacks will actually help them on their way to their bigger goal.

Without blaming the pony, remind the rider that it takes time for the pony to relax within the competition atmosphere, as it does for them. The partnership that has formed in lessons now needs to develop in competition. Sometimes, by turning the focus on the pony, the rider's worries are pushed aside. The concentration on this helps the child to move beyond their own concerns.

Offering your pupils the opportunity to experience small competitions is the perfect introduction to their next aspiration in riding. Goals and aims can be designed around work for competition dates.

11

EXAMS, CERTIFICATES, RALLIES AND COMPETITIONS

Between the Pony Club and the British Horse Society (BHS) there is an enormous wealth of opportunity for both children who do and do not own a pony. If you look at numerous professional riders, you will find that many of them had the opportunity of coming through the excellent grounding given by the Pony Club. Whilst it has safety at the forefront of every activity, it has retained its commitment to honest enjoyment with ponies, which is derived from jolly hard work and steely determination. The humbling experiences of friendship, teamwork, looking after, riding and competing ponies, and the highs and lows associated with them, develop life skills unequalled in any other sport.

As an instructor, you may teach at Pony Club branch rallies or at a Pony Club centre and be able to offer instruction aimed at the Achievement Badges and Tests. At a BHS centre, you may be able to offer Junior Progressive Riding Tests. Or you may teach for the BHS Riding Club affiliated to your centre, which offers tuition and competitions for its junior members.

This chapter aims to give you a guide to ideas, activities and rallies which you can offer children either in association with the BHS and Pony Club, or independently.

THE BRITISH HORSE SOCIETY

The BHS is a leading equine-based charity in the UK. It offers qualifications in equestrianism that are recognised worldwide and has, in the past, been the governing body in the UK for core equestrian sports such as dressage and eventing.

JUNIOR PROGRESSIVE RIDING TESTS

For juniors interested in riding and caring for ponies, the BHS offers the Junior Progressive Riding Tests, which are split into Riding and Stable Management, just like the Stage Exams, and which can be taken separately. This allows a child who is only interested in pony care to progress through the five Levels as readily as one interested in both aspects.

A riding school is able to offer pony owners and child riders who do not own their own pony, training days to learn more about ponies and to work towards a test at the same time. With subjects including safety around horses and ponies, approaching a pony correctly and leading a pony, the syllabus appeals to parents as well as children. The certificates received are well-earned, the children having been tested by an instructor other than their regular one. The instructors must be registered with the BHS, and there are rules on qualifications required in order to examine certain tests.

A stable management lecture in progress.

BHS COMPETITIONS

The BHS can boast a busy competition calendar. Many of the competitions are qualifiers for Championships. Most competitions have junior sections, with a specific competition – Equitation – aimed at young riders who do not have their own ponies. This competition is held at centres throughout the UK and consists of a dressage test, showjumping course and equine related, general knowledge questions. Other competitions include dressage, hunter trials and TREC. TREC is a discipline that originated in France and is steadily growing in popularity elsewhere. It consists of a mixture of orienteering and cross-country.

BHS RIDING CLUBS

There are numerous Riding Clubs in the UK, a large number of which are affiliated to the BHS. Riding Clubs often hold junior activities and have junior

Getting ready for a junior competition.

classes at competitions. They host training clinics, competitions and fun events for riders who wish to enjoy their horses and ponies with other like-minded people. Usually, a Riding Club offers something for everyone – training clinics in dressage, showjumping and cross-country from grass roots level up to affiliated level. Riders will often bring their new mounts up through riding club competitions before affiliating in a discipline. As an instructor involved with the junior section of a Riding Club you may find yourself being asked to teach a group of children about riding on varying terrain in a field, or to teach a clinic on gaining some extra dressage marks in a basic level test. You may be asked to escort a small hack as part of a BBQ ride. The work can be varied and very interesting.

TROT ON CLUB

The Trot on Club (TOC), associated with the BHS, is an interactive website for pony-mad children. Luckily, children who enjoy ponies tend to be active types anyway but, as an instructor, when they are on the computer, you can safely suggest that the younger ones would enjoy testing themselves at the TOC.

THE PONY CLUB

With over 50,000 members in the UK, and over 120,000 worldwide, the Pony Club is a massive family of equestrian enthusiasts, which caters not only for younger children but for young adults up to the age of 21. It has two basic arms, these being Pony Club branches and Pony Club centres. A 'branch' is for children who have a pony with whom they can participate in various activities; a 'centre' is a riding school that has the facilities and instructors to provide activities on riding school ponies. The activities offered include those discussed below. Many are available through both Pony Club branches and centres. However, there may be some practical constraints regarding participation in some activities by children who do not have their own ponies. With this in mind, there is an individual section – Pony Club Centres – later on in this chapter.

RALLIES

Working rallies form the foundation of the Pony Club. These vary in time from a couple of hours to a few days. Pony Club branches usually organise a residential Pony Club camp during the summer holidays, which runs over 4–5 days. This is a fun-filled and progressive time for riders of all levels who take their ponies to camp. They usually sleep over in stables (not usually with ponies in!) or tents. Depending on their level and the facilities available, they enjoy lessons in dressage, showjumping and cross-country. Other activities vary, but can include hacking, mounted games and drill rides and often a competition is held on the last day. Children are taught always to put their ponies first, and on waking, carry out morning stables before their own breakfast. Tack cleaning is marked, as is how well the pony is turned out for lessons. Midnight feasts are a regular for the first night, but most children cannot stay awake past 9pm after that! Rounders and water fights also feature highly on the 'to do' list.

Daily rallies vary in their content, depending on what the children are working towards – stable management, tests or increasing knowledge. Usually they contain a mix of riding and stable management instruction.

Pony Club camps and rallies are sources of fun, and also help riders to progress.

COMPETITION DISCIPLINES

There are so many official disciplines included in the Pony Club, that each child is bound to find at least one that they enjoy participating in. The Pony Club celebrates many of these disciplines at its National Championships which are held over five days and require qualification through regional qualifiers, hosted by Pony Club branches. Pony Club centres are welcome to put forward teams into the qualifiers.

Included are:

Dressage   Tests, including a Walk and Trot test, can be downloaded from the Pony Club website. Training days are available at local branches. There are various Championships to qualify for, including the Pony Club National Championship.

Mounted games in progress.

Endurance Newly adopted as an official discipline with the Pony Club, endurance has its own qualifications and Championship. The rides vary in length between 8 and 15km (about 5–9 miles). The minimum age of rider is 8, and children under 13 must be accompanied by an adult.

Eventing Eventing requires qualification at regional level for the Pony Club National Championship. The website gives dates for area training and competitions.

Mounted Games Mounted games appear at many top shows, including the Royal Windsor, and the Prince Philip Cup is hosted at the Horse of the Year Show.

Polo Polo also has an independent Championship, and qualification is gained through area tournaments. Arena polo is played on an all-weather surface and the team consists of three players.

Polocrosse Through qualifications at regional tournaments, polocrosse teams can qualify for the Pony Club National Championship. A polocrosse team consists of six players, three juniors and three seniors, who alternate chukkas.

Racing There are three different types of pony racing, Pony Club, Racecourse and Point-to-Point. The latter two are organised by the Pony Racing Authority, the governing body for Pony Racing. The ages of riders are between 9 and15 years; the races vary between 4 and 6 furlongs. The ponies are eligible for races by their height: 128cm, 138cm and 148cm (12.2, 13.2 and 14.2 hands) races exist.

Showjumping As with dressage, there are many Championships to qualify for, including the British Open Show Jumping Championship and the Pony Club National Championships. Area competitions include individual and team classes.

Tetrathlon This discipline consists of running, riding, swimming and shooting. The riding phase takes place in a field over cross-country type fences. It also includes opening and closing a gate whilst mounted and dismounting to remove a slip rail, lead the pony through, replace the rail and remount.

TRAINING

The Pony Club aims to promote excellent pony husbandry skills and horsemanship. This begins with a small syllabus for the Mini Achievement Badges all the way to the A Test, which is aimed at the same level as the BHS Stage 4. Exams can be taken for:

- Mini Achievement Badges
- Achievement Badges
- Progressive tests – bronze, silver, gold and platinum – developed for Pony Club Centres
- Tests
  - E standard
  - D standard
  - D+ standard
  - C standard
  - C+ standard
  - Road Rider Test
  - B standard – Horse and Pony care
  - B standard – Riding
  - 2006 Lungeing Test
  - AH Test (Stable Management part of the A Test)
  - A Test
  - Pony Club Hunting Test
  - Polo Tests – Lower and Higher

OTHER TYPES OF COMPETITION

THE PONY CLUB QUIZ

In teams of four, children qualify at regional competitions in order to compete in the National Quiz Final. There are eight rounds of theory, and one newly introduced practical round where juniors guess what fifteen objects are through feel, and seniors test their memory by having 90 seconds to memorise fifteen objects.

THE HORSE AND PONY CARE COMPETITION

Again, through regional qualifiers, teams of three demonstrate their knowledge of equine welfare through a series of questions and practical tasks, along the same lines as the standard tests. The final is held at the annual Pony Club Championship.

A happy Pony Club pony adorned with a well-earned rosette.

PONY CLUB CENTRES

If you teach at a centre, even though the children will not have their own ponies, there are many activities that you can offer your Pony Club members. These include:

- Working rallies – these are where mounted or unmounted instruction is given. They aim to improve the horsemanship and horsemastership of members whilst having fun.
- Training for the Pony Club Quiz. This is one of the simplest ways for a centre to compete alongside branches. Children love learning facts about horses and ponies, and by purchasing and reading the two books in publication of sample questions, training becomes fun.
- Training members for the Horse and Pony Care competitions is also a very popular activity. Since this consists of practical and theoretical sections, it gives a solid foundation to their knowledge. Again, the teams can compete in local qualifying rounds.
- The Achievement Badges, including the Mini Achievement Badges for younger members, are desirable to children. Their aim is to cover their arms in badges, and with the number on offer, this becomes a distinct possibility!
- Progressive Tests (bronze, silver, gold and platinum, each with three levels) are similar to the BHS Progressive Riding Tests. They have a check sheet for children to bring with them each time they ride or attend a rally. Each section contains strong emphasis of safety on the road; potentially life-saving information.
- The Pony Club Test series is also available to all members and can therefore be achieved by centre members.
- Ridden competitions include the National Pony Club Championship, dressage to music and the winter dressage and showjumping leagues.

OTHER IDEAS TO MAKE RIDING FUN

There are plenty of riding schools that offer fun-filled riding opportunities without the overt influence of the BHS or Pony Club. Here are some ideas to make riding fun:

- Play a game at the end of each lesson.
- Have a Rider of the Month award – awarded to the child who has made the most improvement in their riding.
- Also have a Helper of the Month award – for weekend and holiday helpers. This could be given for outstanding pony care or positive attitude.
- Christmas and Easter games. Spend the whole lesson playing games.
- Pony Days – each holiday, offer a day where children can spend the whole day at the yard with activities including riding, stable management, a quiz, a mini competition, gymkhana games and a treasure hunt.
- Picnic hacks – if you have good, safe hacking, picnic hacks are most enjoyable.

12

Stable management

Stable management lessons are of great value to all children, not just pony owners. To gain a basic understanding of equine behaviour most definitely helps children to be more aware and safer around ponies. It also cultivates the love of ponies that inspires most children to start riding in the first place.

If you teach in an outdoor school, stable management lessons can be given on days when the weather is too poor for riding. It can be incorporated into a Pony Day, or take the form of specific lessons to follow the syllabus for a BHS or Pony Club Test or Badge.

A mixture of practical and theory within each session will maintain interest as, although theory is undoubtedly important, most children will favour practical, hands-on experience with the ponies, and almost certainly learn better in that way. Most subjects lend themselves readily to a mixture of both theory and practical.

Topics for study

For each subject below, there is a list of possible topics that could be included. Within these topics, the instructor can offer explanations in as much depth as the age and ability of the child dictates. At the end of the book are example handouts that can be photocopied or used as templates and adapted.

Psychology
Points to include:
- Herd instinct.
- Fight or flight.
- Nomadic.
- Grazers.
- Curiosity.

Making it harder:
- How the ponies' instincts influence their behaviour when we ride.

- How the ponies' instincts influences pony behaviour when we handle them.
- How to catch a difficult pony through knowledge of his instincts.

SAFETY AROUND HORSES AND PONIES

Points to include:
- How ponies shows us how they feel.
- How to approach a pony safely.
- Safe behaviour on the yard.
- Correct clothing to be worn around ponies.

Making it harder:
- How and why different breeds and ages of ponies may react differently.
- Risk assessments – basic analysis of safety around the yard and when handling.
- How to work safely around a pony.

PUTTING ON A HEADCOLLAR, TYING UP AND LEADING

Points to include:
- How to put on a headcollar.
- How to tie up a pony safely.
- How to lead a safe pony correctly.

Making it harder:
- Fitting a headcollar.
- Types of headcollar.
- Different methods of restraint.

POINTS OF A PONY

Points to include:
- Basic points of a pony.

Making it harder:
- Additional points.

RUGS

Points to include:
- Stable, New Zealand and cooler rugs.
- Putting on a rug.
- Fastenings.

Making it harder:

- Fitting a rug.
- Rug measurements.
- Washing and storing rugs.

GROOMING

Points to include:

- Basic items of the grooming kit.
- Uses of basic brushes.
- How to pick out feet.
- How to give basic grooming.

Making it harder:

- Names and uses of the complete grooming kit.
- Reasons for grooming.
- Knowing what the term 'strapping' means and how to groom a pony thoroughly.

TACKING UP

Points to include:

- Parts of the bridle.
- Parts of the saddle.
- Different types of numnahs.
- How to tack up safely.

Making it harder:

- Martingales and breastplates.
- Fitting a snaffle bridle.
- Fitting a saddle.

COLOURS AND MARKINGS

Points to include:

- Basic colours.
- Basic markings.

Making it harder:

- All colours.
- All markings.

RULES OF FEEDING AND WATERING

Points to include:

- Ten rules of feeding and reasons for the rules.
- Rules of watering and reasons for the rules.

Making it harder:

- Feeding the grass-kept pony.

DIFFERENT TYPES OF FEED

Points to include:

- Basic foods – grass, hay, succulents.

Making it harder:

- Different grains.
- The difference between compounds and straights.

> **See handouts at the end of the book.**

13

PROBLEM-SOLVING

Hopefully, most of your experiences as a riding instructor will be pleasant and fulfilling, but it would be unrealistic to pretend that problematic situations will never arise. In this chapter we will consider some potential difficulties and ways of coping with them.

REMAINING CALM IN DIFFICULT SITUATIONS

As a riding instructor, there are many situations in which you might find yourself which make you feel uncomfortable. These could include:

■ Rider falls.
■ Pony falls.
■ Parents who are difficult to deal with.
■ Riders who are difficult to deal with.
■ Other people letting you down.
■ Being unsure what decision to make.

First, from a very clinical and self-developmental point of view, being taken out of your comfort zone offers you the opportunity to learn something new. This may not happen at the time, but with hindsight you might see a different way to handle a similar situation in the future. This is part of development, and no one handles every situation perfectly every time, but we learn for next time.

Very importantly, remain calm. Although adrenalin usually helps in performance, only remaining calm will allow you to think clearly. Remaining calm also prevents a difficult situation from becoming heated, or making a snap decision that you may regret later. Try to assess the problem logically and think of a logical solution.

You may already have a coping strategy for difficult situations. If not, think about some of these:

- Do not take comments personally.
- Thank people for their comments – this often diffuses a situation.
- Give yourself breathing space – even a few seconds may give you enough clarity to deal correctly with the situation. If you require more time, thank the person concerned for their comments and tell them you will contact them once you have had time to consider. Ensure that you follow this through, without unnecessary delay.
- Try to handle problems discreetly.
- Think about potentially difficult situations in advance and plan how you would handle them, allowing for variations.
- Think about how someone you admire would handle the situation.
- Ask for help and advice.

MANAGING DIFFICULT PARENTS AND CARERS

We are fortunate in this industry that we mainly deal with parents who want the best for their children. Inevitably, however, difficult situations arise that will require delicate handling. The strategy for dealing with such situations clearly includes the need to keep calm as mentioned above. In this way, you retain a professional persona and can think more clearly. Here are some more pointers for dealing with such situations:

- Be polite and discreet: talk in private.
- Listen to their concerns: people often calm down once their point has been heard.
- Be confident enough to take comments on board if they have validity and to modify your thoughts.
- When you have a strong belief, politely stand your ground.
- As mentioned earlier, if you are not good at thinking on your feet, thank them for their comments and say you will come back to them once you have had time to consider. You may only need a couple of minutes, but do not be forced into a snap decision.

DEALING WITH NERVOUSNESS

We all have a threshold for nervousness. Nerves are not always rational, but they must be dealt with. As an instructor, it is very useful to learn a new skill yourself, so you are, in effect, 'stepping into a pupil's shoes'. Training people in a subject in which we are comfortable and competent can make us complacent and less sympathetic to others' fears. By learning a new skill ourselves, we get a reminder of how hard it is to follow instructions and co-ordinate our movements. If the new skill is physical, and potentially dangerous, we will all reach a point of nervousness. There are many reasons that can contribute to this feeling, for example:

- The subject was introduced in a way which made it appear difficult, setting up a negative feeling.
- Overheard a negative conversation.
- Had a bad first experience, even physical discomfort.
- Seeing someone else have a bad experience: fears adopted from others.
- Realistic concerns about a potentially dangerous activity.

All these points are valid reasons for a rider to become nervous. In addition, as riders we are dealing with animals with minds of their own, adding another element of uncertainty.

The new experience of riding outside is one reason why a pupil may feel nervous. A good instructor will always be sensitive to signs of nervousness and seek ways to resolve the issue.

Always try to find the root cause of a pupil's nerves and resolve this issue. The child may feel pressurised to achieve a goal that they consider beyond their current ability. They may have had a bad riding experience and have valid concerns about a repeat. Once the reason for nervousness is discovered, you may be able to allay the rider's fears. For example, an unusual accident is unlikely to happen again and you can explain this; perhaps another rider may have deliberately tried to scare a younger child, and again, you can correct this. (Do try to speak with the child responsible, with the parent(s) of the child present.)

An instructor is in an interesting position. The remedy for nerves is confidence, and the instructor must know how to handle each child as an individual in order to achieve that. One child may gain confidence from gentle persuasion to have a go, another from a 'get on with it' attitude, and another from watching others achieve before they develop the courage to try for themselves.

Always remember the duty of care. Even (or most especially) in our results-driven society, it is important to wait until the child is ready, curious and asks to try the next step. This positive attitude is more likely to set them up for success, upon which they will build. Work at the child's pace, and be confident yourself that they will succeed. There is always another day.

Sometimes, it is the parents, not the child, who feel the nerves. A little discussion can reveal this, at which point the effect on the child can be gently pointed out. Usually the parents will suggest that they stop watching for a while, which is the best idea as it allows the child the freedom to progress.

WHAT TO DO IN THE EVENT OF A FALL

Having taken the First Aid At Work certificate, you will remember your training immediately:

Assess the situation
Prevent further accidents
Assess the casualty
Call for help

Assess the situation – Where are you? Where is the child? The pony? How many are involved? Where are the other riders? Are you on your own?

Prevent further accidents – Having assessed the situation, prevent any further accidents from happening. Halt the ride in the school. Catch the pony if he may cause another accident by being free. You may need to call for help at this point to prevent other accidents. Calm the children down. Give them a task. They must stand still and reassure their ponies. By taking control of the situation, you give the children the confidence in your ability to keep them safe.

Assess the casualty – Follow your first aid training. Ensure that you do not move the casualty too quickly, even if the fall looked innocuous. Give them time. For falls where the young riders are fine and on their feet straight away, try not to make a big deal out of it. Falls happen; it is a part of riding. On they jump again, to be told how they can avoid it in the future.

However much care is taken all round, the possibility remains that riders may sometimes have falls. An instructor must be properly prepared to respond to such occurrences in an appropriate manner.

Call for help – If the child needs medical help, this must be called for immediately. If the child needs a little time to recover, you will need someone to help you, either to look after the child, or to continue with the lesson. If you are not yet a first aider and you have the slightest thought that the child might have hurt themselves, in ANY way, call the first aider on duty.

ISSUES WITH INDIVIDUAL CHILDREN
BEHAVIOUR THAT THREATENS THE SAFETY OR ENJOYMENT OF OTHERS

Your responsibility is for the safety of all the children in your care. If a rider's actions threaten the safety of others, you must take action. Usually, in a riding school, this behaviour is going to manifest itself in high spirits during a lesson, where children can make their ponies excited, and therefore threaten the safety of the class. A simple explanation and/or change of exercise usually resolves the problem.

If there is a child who is constantly disruptive within the lesson, there are a few things to try:

- Discuss the problem with the parents – it is likely that such a child is disruptive at school also, and they may be able to offer you advice about the best way of management. You do need to gauge whether you have parental support – this is very important. Quite possibly, they are using riding as a carrot for good behaviour, so they will want to work with you.
- Put the rider on ponies that offer greater or lesser challenges, depending on the reason for the bad behaviour.
- Give the rider more/less attention.
- Give the rider more/less praise.
- Discipline appropriately – for example, stand the child still in the middle of the school for a period. Ensure that warnings are given first so that the child understands there will be consequences for the actions, then follow through if necessary.
- Put the child into a different group, where they will be the strongest/weakest – again, dependent on the reason for the disruption.

BULLYING
Occasionally, there may be bullying within a riding school. Be very clear that you do not tolerate bullying. Let the children know that they may confide in you if they wish to, and that they are all here to enjoy riding. If it continues, discuss the situation with the parents. The children may come from the same school, and there may possibly be a procedure that the school has in place that would work

during their time at the yard also. The most obvious solution is to separate the children into different classes, preferably on different days. Although this does not tackle the issue head-on, it will solve the problem within that group.

THE CHILD WHOSE OWN PONY IS UNSUITABLE

Sadly, when parents buy their child's first pony, they often do not take advice and purchase a youngster they think that the child will 'grow into'. If they are lucky, this will happen. Often, however, an instructor will be called in once there is a problem. Once the situation has been assessed – rider, pony, parents, facilities, aims – the instructor can offer their professional opinion regarding the pony. While you may be able to help the combination, there may be times when you have to offer the advice that another pony is sought, or that the pony undertakes regular schooling with a more experienced rider to help his development.

THE CHILD WHO NEEDS A GREATER CHALLENGE

OUTGROWN PONY

This section looks first at a different form of 'unsuitability' from that dealt with above. In this case, we are looking at a pony who might have been eminently suitable for a while, but through no fault of his own, is no longer so. If a child has their own pony and they have outgrown the pony, whether physically, in terms of their increasing ability, or both, then a discussion has to take place with the parents to that effect. There are choices here – they could sell or loan the pony; they could keep the pony and buy the next one; or they could keep the first pony and loan a new one. Children grow and progress quickly when they have their own, initially suitable pony, and it can be a difficult situation all round when a favourite pony is outgrown. One way in which you, as an instructor, may be able to help resolve the issue is that, through your contacts, you may be in a position to recommend a good new home for the outgrown pony, and perhaps be aware of a replacement who may be suitable to enable your pupil to progress.

BALANCING SPEED OF PROGRESSION

By being mindful that we should not put children under too much pressure, we are sometimes guilty of not managing their progress swiftly enough. If this is identified as a problem, it can be quickly remedied. However, we should be careful not to switch from 'too slow' to 'too fast'.

Another problem that can arise in training is that sometimes, when a child focuses on one discipline, staleness can set in. In such a case, the next challenge could include some cross-training with another discipline to inject freshness into the child, the pony and the instructor.

CHILDREN WITH LEARNING DIFFICULTIES

In addition to a better understanding nowadays that children generally learn at different speeds and in different styles, there is also greater recognition of learning difficulties. Having a clinical diagnosis of a learning difficulty aids the instructor to teach the child concerned in the best possible method with the best explanations. Sadly, there still remains a stigma attached to learning difficulties and you may find that the parents do not wish to disclose the difficulty to you, even to the extent that they will omit to answer the question on the rider registration form.

If you suspect, but cannot be certain, that a child has learning difficulties, use whatever knowledge you have in order to teach the child to the best of your ability. Seek advice from more experienced instructors on how to ascertain information discreetly from the parents as to whether there is a learning difficulty. Usually you can simply ask if there is any way you can explain instructions better.

THE CHILD WHO WANTS TO GIVE UP RIDING

It is a part of childhood development that children should be exposed to many different activities. Inevitably, some they will continue, some they will give up – and this may include riding. If you, as the instructor can, hand on heart, confirm to yourself that you have delivered enjoyable, interesting and instructive lessons on suitable ponies, then do not take this personally – bear in mind that the child may return to riding in the future with renewed enthusiasm. If you feel that you could have done better in any way, try to do so before the child gives up. Reflection of our abilities as an instructor develops us further and will help us teach in the future.

CONCLUSION

Teaching children to ride can be one of the most rewarding experiences gained from teaching in the equestrian industry. Your ability to impart your knowledge and passion for horses and ponies can inspire the next generation of young riders, and help to mould the future of a young person. Safety is always of paramount importance, closely followed by the enjoyment of the sport, and improving the rider (and pony).

From information given at the time of booking, to first lessons and subsequently developing the rider to the level that they desire to reach – or even beyond – the instructor plays an important role, not only in teaching children how to ride, but giving them the confidence to make each progressive step. Each rider has different goals, and a good teacher knows that their personal aspirations are not always shared by their riders. We can all remember the teachers at school who most inspired us, even if it was not within our favourite subject. By offering a broad knowledge and supporting riders in whichever way they wish to enjoy equestrian activities, we work towards fulfilling the instructor's role.

USEFUL CONTACTS

Pony Club Stoneleigh Park, Kenilworth, Warwickshire CV8 2RW
Tel: 02476 698300 • Website: www.pcuk.org • Email: enquiries@pcuk.org

British Horse Society, Stoneleigh Deer Park, Kenilworth, Warwickshire CV8 2XZ
Tel: 0844 848 1666 • Website: www.bhs.org.uk • Email: enquiry@bhs.org.uk

British Equestrian Federation, Stoneleigh Park, Kenilworth, Warwickshire CV8 2RH
Tel: 02476 698871 • Website: www.bef.co.uk • Email: info@bef.co.uk

British Dressage, Stoneleigh Park, Kenilworth, Warwickshire, CV8 2RJ
Tel: 02476 698830 • Website: www.britishdressage.co.uk
Email: office@britishdressage.co.uk

British Eventing, Stoneleigh Park, Kenilworth, Warwickshire CV8 2RN
Tel: 0845 262 3344 • Website: www.britisheventing.co.uk
Email: info@britisheventing.com

British Showjumping, National Agricultural Centre, Stoneleigh Park, Kenilworth, Warwickshire, CV8 2LR Tel: 024 7669 8800 • Website: www.britishshowjumping.co.uk • Email: enquiry contacts available on website

Endurance GB, National Agricultural Centre, Stoneleigh Park, Kenilworth, Warwickshire, CV8 2RP Tel: 02476 697929 • Website: endurancegb.co.uk
Email: enquiries@endurancegb.co.uk

APPENDIX – TABLE OF DISTANCES

DISTANCES IN GRIDS AND COMBINATIONS

The *ideal* distances for any pony will vary according to a number of factors, including natural length of stride, temperament, ground conditions, type and siting of fences and how the pony is ridden. However, course-builders and instructors generally have to accommodate a number of ponies and their riders and thus have to work on the basis of sensible average distances.

The distances below are reasonable distances for ponies of ordinary ability jumping fences of modest size (i.e. around 84cm/2ft 9in), with the approach in canter.

TABLE OF DISTANCES – ONE NON-JUMPING STRIDE

Pony size	1 Stride	Metres	Feet
128cm/12.2hh	1	6.1–6.4	20–21
138cm/13.2hh	1	6.4–6.7	21–22
148cm/14.2hh	1	6.7–7.0	22–23

For additional non-jumping strides between elements, add approximately the following distances for each non-jumping stride:

		Metres	Feet
128cm/12.2hh pony	–	2.7–3.1	9–10
138cm/13.2hh pony	–	3.1–3.2	10–10½
148cm/14.2hh pony	–	3.3–3.5	11–11½

The more strides there are between elements, the more scope there will be for a pony to adjust his stride – however, remember that the ideal is for the length and rhythm of stride to remain constant, so every effort should be made to provide distances that help achieve this. The exception to this principle is when a grid of jumps is approached in trot, with the intention that, having jumped the first element, the pony will pick up canter. In this case, the distance between the first two elements should be rather shorter than for an approach in canter, because the pony, jumping from trot, will make less ground over the first element.

SIMPLE QUESTIONS

1 **Write down the term we use to describe each of the pony's natural instincts explained below.**

The pony lives in a group in a field. The group stick together and react together.
(Term) _____

Ponies' natural reaction to danger is to run away. If they cannot run away, they will defend themselves. *(Term)* _____

In the wild, ponies wander over large areas of land, seeking food and water.
(Term) _____

The pony's digestive system is suited to eating almost continuously and the pony is kept mentally healthy from chewing. *(Term)* _____

Ponies show an interest in everything. *(Term)* _____

2 **How have we changed the lifestyle of ponies by keeping them in stables?**

_____

_____

_____

_____

_____

HARDER QUESTIONS

1 The pony has several natural instincts. Beside each of the instincts listed below, write down how they may influence the pony in the stable or when ridden.

Herd instinct _____
_____
_____
_____

Fight or flight _____
_____
_____
_____

Nomadic _____
_____
_____
_____

Grazers _____
_____
_____
_____

Curiosity _____
_____
_____
_____

2 Describe how you could use the pony's curiosity to help to catch a difficult pony.
_____
_____
_____
_____

SIMPLE QUESTIONS

1 The following pictures show ponies looking happy, unwell and angry. Label which is which.

2 The statements below about safety around the yard are either right or wrong. Can you tell which is which?

You should not wear jewellery around ponies.   RIGHT / WRONG

Shouting on the yard may scare ponies.   RIGHT / WRONG

Running on the yard is safe.   RIGHT / WRONG

Playing on hay or straw bales is unsafe.   RIGHT / WRONG

Tools should be stored neatly, away from the ponies.   RIGHT / WRONG

3 The rider shown here is incorrectly dressed for the yard. Circle as many wrong items of clothing as you can.

HARDER QUESTIONS

1 The picture below shows a dangerous yard. Circle as many hazards as you can.

2 Produce a risk assessment of all the good and bad points of safety on your yard.

Good: _____

_____

_____

_____

_____

_____

_____

Bad: _____

_____

_____

_____

_____

_____

_____

HANDOUT: HEADCOLLAR, TYING UP AND LEADING

SIMPLE QUESTIONS

1 Describe how to put on a headcollar:

2 Why do we tie the pony to baler twine and not directly to the tie ring?

3 The two pictures below show a pony being led. One shows the pony being led correctly, the other incorrectly. Beside each picture, write down what is correct about the first picture, and what is wrong with the second picture.

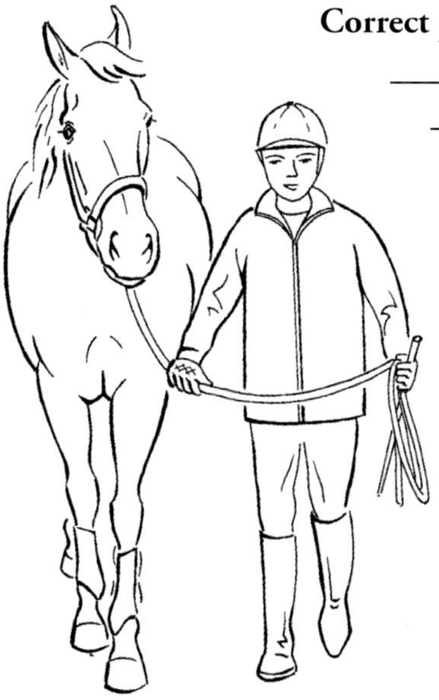

Correct points:

Incorrect points:

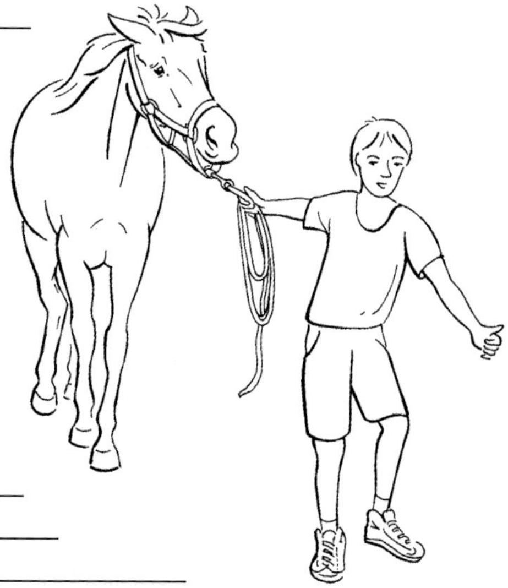

Handout: HEADCOLLAR, TYING UP AND LEADING

Harder questions

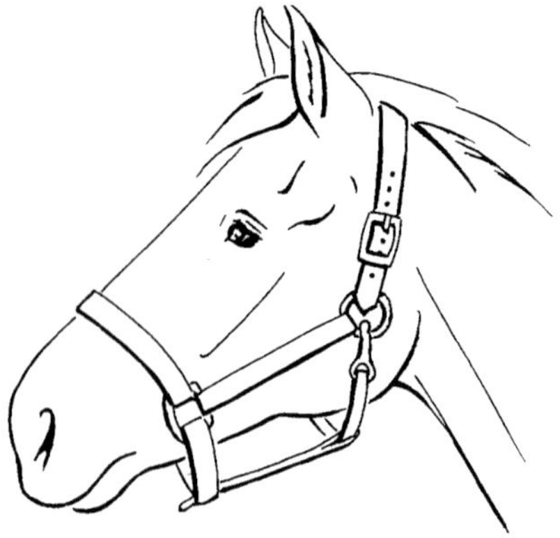

1 The picture on the right shows a well-fitting headcollar. What points should you remember when fitting a headcollar?

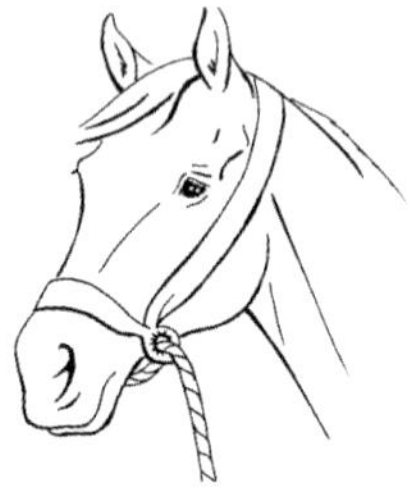

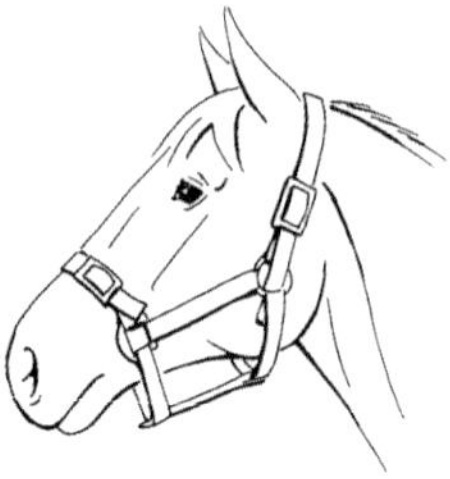

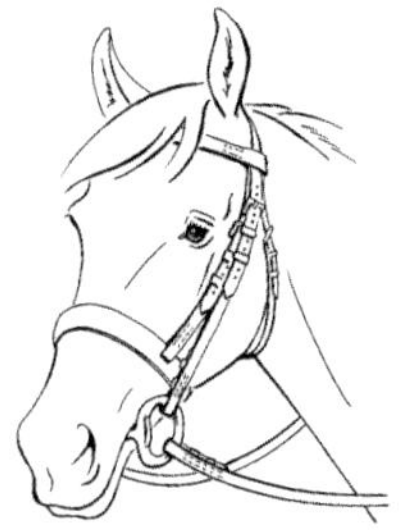

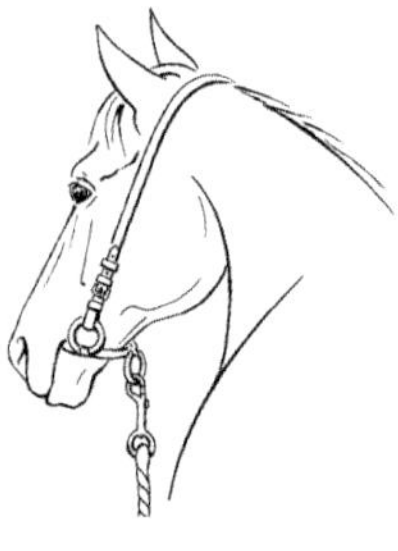

2 The following pictures show different methods of restraint. Name them and give an example of when they might be used.

SIMPLE QUESTIONS

1 On the picture below, label the following points of the pony:
   head, eye, nose, ears, mouth, neck, mane, back, tail, foreleg, hind leg, hoof.

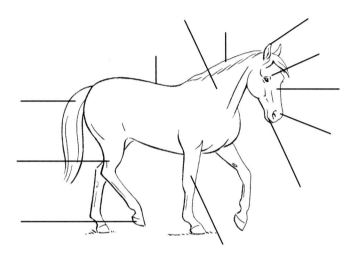

HARDER QUESTIONS

1 On the picture below, label the following points of the pony: poll, shoulder, withers, croup, dock, thigh, stifle, point of hock, heel, fetlock, pastern, cannon bone, knee, elbow, chin groove.

Simple questions

1 **Describe when you would use each of the rugs listed below.**

Stable   _____

                     _____

New Zealand   _____

                     _____

Cooler   _____

                     _____

2 **Circle 'true' or 'false' to each of the statements below about putting on a rug.**

You must always tie a pony up to put on a rug: TRUE / FALSE

The fastenings should always be tied up securely before putting on the rug: TRUE/ FALSE

The rug should be placed over the hindquarters of the pony first: TRUE / FALSE

Rugs keep ponies warm in the winter: TRUE / FALSE

The rug is folded correctly before being put on the pony: TRUE / FALSE

3 **Using the following words, fill in the gaps of the paragraph about rug fastenings.**

back   *breaks*   *tail*   *surcingle*   *strap*   *fillet*   *chest*

There are usually two front straps on the rug that fit around the pony's .... By using two straps, if one of the straps ...., the rug will still be held in position and not slip backwards. The rug is fastened under the belly by .... straps, again usually two of them. The end of the rug can be secured by either a .... string, which lies beneath the pony's ...., or by leg straps. Each leg .... links through the other, to fasten back on to the rug, securing the .... of the rug.

HARDER QUESTIONS

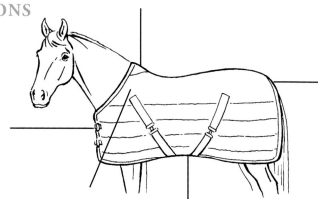

1 **The picture above shows a well-fitting rug. On each label, describe the points to look for at that part of the rug.**

2 **(a) In what units are rugs measured?**

   (b) In what increments do rug sizes go up?

   (c) Give an example of a common rug size for a pony.

3 **Using the words below, fill in the gaps of the paragraph about washing and storing rugs.**

*repaired   cleaned   dry   pony   skin   moth balls   dirty
industrial   re-waterproofed   New Zealand*

Rugs will need to be .... periodically during their time of use. This is to ensure that the .... remains clean and does not develop any .... conditions from wearing a .... rug. Once the rugs are no longer needed, they should be cleaned and stored safely in a .... environment. They can sometimes be cleaned in an .... washing machine on the yard, or through a rug cleaning company. .... rugs may need to be .... annually, depending on the material that they are made from. Rugs will also need to be .... before storage. Putting .... into the rug container will prevent them from being damaged by moths whilst in storage.

SIMPLE QUESTIONS

1 Name the items of grooming kit in the pictures below.

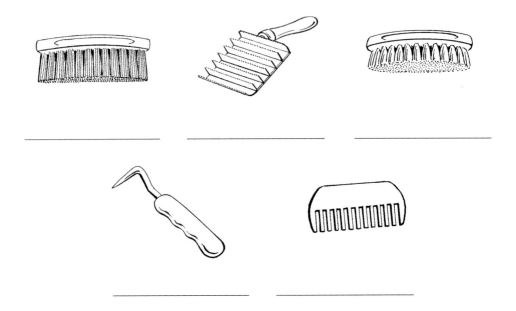

2 Which item of grooming kit must never be used on a pony's body?

_____

3 On the picture of the pony below, label which item of the grooming kit in question 1 you would use on each of these parts: mane, body, foot.

HARDER QUESTIONS

1 Describe the use of each part of the grooming kit listed below.

Hoofpick _____

_____

Body brush _____

_____

Dandy brush _____

_____

Metal curry comb _____

_____

Plastic curry comb _____

_____

Rubber curry comb _____

_____

Water brush _____

_____

Mane comb _____

_____

Stable rubber _____

_____

Sponge _____

_____

Wisp _____

_____

Face brush _____

_____

2 List three reasons for grooming:

(1) _____

(2) _____

(3) _____

3 **Using the words below, fill in the gaps in the paragraph about grooming a pony thoroughly.**

stable rubber   scrubbing   dry   brush   wisped   clipped   body   head
mane comb   de-tangled   sponge   tied   dock   unclipped   regulate

The pony should be correctly .... Begin by picking out and .... the pony's feet with water. These can then .... whilst the rest of the pony is groomed. Select the appropriate .... for the pony's body depending on whether the pony lives in or out and is .... or not. Brush the neck, ... and legs. When brushing the head, the pony should be .... from the lead-rope for safety. Using the face brush, groom the .... of the pony. Use the .... to tidy the mane. The tail, if it is clean can be .... using your fingers. The eyes and nose should be gently cleaned with a damp ...., and a different sponge used for the .... A fit pony can be ....on the muscular parts of his body. Grooming is finished off by using a .... to lightly remove the surface dust and the hooves oiled using a light oil that does not affect the ability of the hoof to .... moisture levels.

4 **Grooming thoroughly gives you the chance to notice things that may be wrong with the pony. On the picture below, label problems you might notice in the areas indicated.**

SIMPLE QUESTIONS

1 **Label all the parts of the bridle
in the picture.**

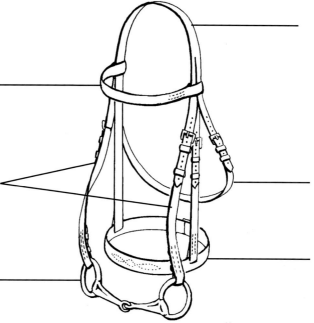

2 **Label all the parts of the saddle in the picture.**

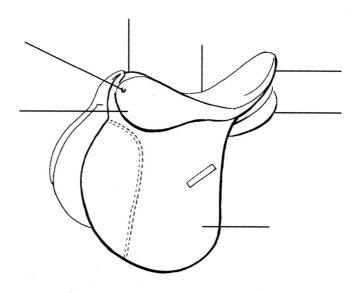

HARDER QUESTIONS

1 **The picture below shows a correctly fitted snaffle bridle. At each label, describe what you look for to fit that part correctly.**

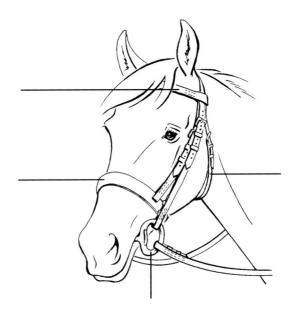

2 **It is very important that a saddle fits the pony correctly, so that he can work freely and comfortably. Circle 'true' of 'false' for each of the statements about saddle fit:**

The cantle should rock up and down on the pony's back: TRUE / FALSE

The saddle should only fit with the girth done up tight: TRUE / FALSE

The saddle arch should not press on the pony's spine: TRUE / FALSE

The saddle should tip down from back to front: TRUE / FALSE

Saddles sometimes need adjusting if the pony has changed shape: TRUE / FALSE

If a saddle is too narrow, adding a numnah will improve the fit: TRUE / FALSE

SIMPLE QUESTIONS

1 **Give the correct colour for the descriptions below.**

Brown body with black mane and tail _____

Ginger body, mane and tail _____

White body, mane and tail _____

2 **Write the correct name under each of the markings below.**

HARDER QUESTIONS

1 **Give the correct colour for the descriptions below.**
Sandy body with a black mane and tail _____
Chestnut body with a cream mane and tail _____
Grey body, mane and tail with flecks of chestnut throughout

_____

2 **Write the correct name under each of these markings.**

SIMPLE QUESTIONS

1 **Under each of the ten rules of feeding, write the reason for the rule.**

Give the correct amount of feed for the pony ————————————

————————————————————————————————————

Give good quality feedstuff ——————————————————

————————————————————————————————————

The feed room and mangers must be kept clean ————————

————————————————————————————————————

Feed in a routine ——————————————————————

————————————————————————————————————

Make no sudden changes to the diet ————————————

————————————————————————————————————

Feed succulents daily ————————————————————

————————————————————————————————————

The diet should have a high fibre content ————————————

————————————————————————————————————

Feed little and often ————————————————————

————————————————————————————————————

Do not feed directly before or directly after exercise ——————

————————————————————————————————————

Do not water directly after feeding ————————————

————————————————————————————————————

2 **Under each of the rules of watering, list the reasons for the rule.**

Offer the pony a continuous supply of fresh, clean water ————

————————————————————————————————————

Water before feeding ————————————————————

————————————————————————————————————

Never allow the pony to drink a large amount immediately after hard exercise
when he is hot ————————————————————————

————————————————————————————————————

Do not work the pony straight after a large drink ——————

————————————————————————————————————

Keep water containers clean, and they should be deep enough for
a good draught ——————————————————————

————————————————————————————————————

HARDER QUESTIONS

1 The pictures below show a pony living at grass in summer and winter. Under each picture, describe how you might feed a pony in the summer and winter.

_____

_____

_____

_____

_____

_____

_____

_____

HANDOUT: DIFFERENT TYPES OF FEED

SIMPLE QUESTIONS

1 What is the most natural food that a pony eats? ____________

2 In winter, we feed the pony dried grass. What is this called? ____________

3 What is a succulent? ____________

4 Why do we feed succulents? ____________

5 List succulents that you could feed to a pony ____________

____

HARDER QUESTIONS

1 What is a grain? ____________

2 Write a simple description of what each of the feeds listed below looks like.

Oats ____________

Barley ____________

Bran ____________

Sugar beet – both before and after soaking ____________

____

Chaff ____________

3 What is the difference between a compound and a straight feed?

____

____

____

____

INDEX